Interpreting Site

Interpreting Site explains the basic methods you can use to translate what you perceive to represent the complex conditions that physically and mentally "construe" a site, helping you to shape your final design. Within each of the four themes—defining site, experiencing site, spatializing site, and site as system— you are introduced to theoretical, conceptual, and analytic methods and representational tools to give you a foundation to develop your own approach to the conditions of a site. Author Genevieve S. Baudoin pits longstanding represent-ation methods against emerging and experimental methods to give you an idiosyncratic and provocative look at different approaches.

Four case studies of key contemporary projects in Spain, the United States, the United Kingdom, and Norway illustrate how architects have used conditions discovered on a site in their final design.

Genevieve S. Baudoin is an Assistant Professor at the College of Architecture, Planning and Design at Kansas State University, in Manhattan, Kansas, USA. She is also a registered architect in the state of New Mexico, and the co-founder of the collaborative design practice Dual Ecologies.

"A book that contemplates drawing and representation as means of conceiving place through site is unprecedented and timely."

Bruce Johnson, Assistant Professor, The University of Kansas
School of Architecture, Design and Planning, USA

Interpreting Site

Studies in Perception,
Representation, and Design

Genevieve S. Baudoin

Routledge
Taylor & Francis Group

NEW YORK AND LONDON

First published 2016
by Routledge
711 Third Avenue, New York, NY 10017

and by Routledge
2 Park Square, Milton Park, Abingdon, Oxon OX14 4RN

Routledge is an imprint of the Taylor & Francis Group, an informa business

Library of Congress Cataloguing in Publication Data
Baudoin, Genevieve.
Interpreting site : studies in perception, representation, and design / Genevieve Baudoin.
pages cm
Includes bibliographical references and index.
1. Building sites–Planning. 2. Architectural design. I. Title.
NA2540.5.B38 2015
720.28–dc23
2014037940

ISBN: 978-1-138-02069-6 (hbk)
ISBN: 978-1-138-02077-1 (pbk)
ISBN: 978-1-315-77815-0 (ebk)

Acquisition editor: Wendy Fuller
Editorial assistant: Grace Harrison
Production editor: Ed Gibbons

Typeset in Univers
by Fish Books Ltd.

Contents

Acknowledgements

This book would not have been possible without the generosity and support of Kansas State University and the School of Architecture, Design and Planning who provided the space (both literal and figurative) to tackle this project, and the support of both colleagues and administration there. In addition, the students I have been privileged to teach have been a vital springboard for my own thinking at that institution, as well as the University of Kansas and the University of New Mexico. I would also like to acknowledge all of the architects, authors, designers, and photographers who helped to create this book—there are too many to individually acknowledge here, but I am grateful for your support and contributions. Specifically, I would like to acknowledge and thank Wendy Fuller at Routledge for taking me on, Jeffrey Balmer for suggesting it, and Grace Harrison for being a tireless editor along the way. I would also never have been able to start this project without Christopher Mead—thank you for your wisdom, the possibility of having both a mentor and collaborator, and for always being willing to enter into a debate. And to my family and husband—thank you, I would not be me without you.

Foreword

Christopher C. Mead

Place and site are symbiotic: a building turns a place into a site in order to make a place. Categorically different yet practically dependent, place and site are like the orchid and the wasp described by Gilles Deleuze. According to Deleuze, the plant and insect *territorialize* each other: the orchid attracts the wasp by "reproducing its image," and the wasp in turn reproduces "the orchid by transporting its pollen."[1] Formal imitation yields to the more formative effects of genetic exchange, in an open-ended process of territorial becoming. The spatial metaphor applies as well to architecture, and indicates how the act of building at once reproduces a site and makes the building site a territorial intermediary between places.

For some time, Genevieve Baudoin and I have each been thinking—she as an architect and I as an historian—about this exchange and its consequences. When, in the Spring 2011, I was asked to develop and teach a new course called *Architecture and Context* at the University of New Mexico, I invited her to be my colleague and collaborator on the project. We agreed that if "context" were to define "architecture," then the assigned descriptor should be freed at once from its implied restriction to forms of historical imitation, and from the belief that context was fixed and inherent in things. To us, context was not only a multivalent concept with multiple meanings, but also something actively made, not passively inherited: to use an architectural metaphor, context is *constructed* both conceptually and physically. Our framing of context in dynamic terms of change challenged the popular perception that architectural context in New Mexico is defined by the supposedly unchanging adobe forms of its Pueblo and Spanish Colonial traditions. But we had more in mind than the actual variability and historical instability of a place that extends from the epochal ruins of Chaco

Canyon to the nuclear transience of Trinity Site. More generally, we were interested in how the practice and theory of architecture has shifted since the Industrial Revolution, from the classical realm of self-contained monuments, to contingent and fragmentary interventions into the complex systems (of space, infrastructure, information, etc.) that increasingly characterize our world. In response, we positioned context in the conceptual space between Simon Unwin's formulation of architecture as coherently composed objects grounded in a place, and Stan Allen's counter-formulation of architecture as fluctuating spatio-temporal matrices that he called field conditions.[2]

Genevieve Baudoin has since moved on to other universities, where she has developed subsequent generations of the course that we first taught together in 2011. The present book is the result of her evolving investigations. While it contains traces of our initial collaboration—in, for example, the continued use of Unwin and Allen—its structure and content are far removed from where we began. The semantic shift of the book's title, from the generality of context to the specificity of site as a formative condition of architecture, speaks not only of the architect's attention to the pragmatics of design, but also of her critical independence: where *context* carries connotations of place that can obstruct original thought, *site* is an indexical term whose connotative neutrality leaves it open to fresh analysis. The book's distance from its genetic origins is consistent with a course that we meant to be experimental and provisional, an open-ended investigation of possibilities that encourage critical thinking, rather than a closed statement of canonic principles that reinforce conventional wisdom.

Yet even as this territorial exchange generates new conceptual spaces for the making of architecture, it confirms the preoccupations found at the center of Baudoin's book. The first preoccupation is the fraught exchange in architecture between site and place, between the representational space that an architect construes in the process of designing a building and the actual spaces of a building that we experience collectively over time. Martin Heidegger recognized this distinction when he identified two kinds of space in "Building Dwelling Thinking": bounded space, which he named with the German word *Raum*, meaning the space of dwelling and therefore a place; and abstract space, which he named with the Latin word *spatium*, meaning space measured by mathematical intervals and therefore a site.[3] Because architects do not have Heidegger's philosophical luxury of preferring *Raum* over *spatium*, place over site, they must negotiate the territory between these spaces, representing a site in order to make a place for experience.

The second preoccupation is architecture's equally fraught exchange between drawing and building. Ever since the craft of building was redefined in the Renaissance as the art of design—after *disegno*, the Italian word for drawing—theorists from Leon Battista Alberti up to Robin Evans, Juhanni Pallasmaa, and Marco Frascari have sought to explain the profession's reliance on drawing. If, as Frascari said, drawings "make architectural thinking possible" and thus allow architects to conceive complex physical objects through the projective act of design, they do so with a figurative and two-dimensional medium whose representational logic is alien to the constructive and three-dimensional logic of buildings.[4] Just as site makes possible but cannot be a place, so drawing makes possible but cannot be a building.

Interpreting Site takes us deep into this territory of the wasp and the orchid called architecture. Wisely, Genevieve Baudoin avoids the temptation to be comprehensive, offering instead what she says is an idiosyncratic, open-ended discourse on both established and emerging methods of site analysis and representation. She knows that any answers to our questions are conditional, and she intends her critical insights and perceptive case studies to provoke further questions, further investigations, further generations of ideas. Follow her and you will learn to see with your mind, which is where architecture begins.

Notes

1   Gilles Deleuze, "Rhizome Versus Trees," in *The Deleuze Reader*, ed. Constanin V. Boundas (New York: Columbia University Press, 1993), 32.

2   Simon Unwin, *Analysing Architecture*, 3rd edition (London: Routledge, 2009); Stan Allen, "Field Conditions," *Points and Lines: Diagrams and Projects for the City* (New York: Princeton Architectural Press, 1999).

3   Martin Heidegger, "Building Dwelling Thinking," *Poetry, Language, Thought*, trans. A. Hofstadter (New York: Harper & Row, 1971), 145–161.

4   Marco Frascari, *Eleven Exercises in the Art of Architectural Drawing: Slow Food for the Architect's Imagination* (London: Routledge, 2011), 9. See also Leon Battista Alberti, *On the Art of Building in Ten Books*, trans. J. Rykwert, N. Leach, and R. Tavernor (Cambridge, MA: MIT Press, 1988); Robin Evans, "Translations from Drawing to Building," *Translations from Drawing to Building and Other Essays* (London: Architectural Association, 1997), 152–193; Juhanni Pallasmaa, *The Thinking Hand: Existential and Embodied Wisdom in Architecture* (Chichester: John Wiley & Sons, 2009).

Introduction

The ubiquitous site visit, traditionally entailing physical displacement to an actual place in order to observe its context and conditions, might now mean observing various phenomena related to site— anything from analyzing a televised spectacle to dissecting an object or deconstructing a text. From this systematic re-reading of the site an implicit re-writing takes place, which of course includes re-present- ation of the given program for a proposed building.

Hani Rashid and Lise Anne Couture[1]

Site, in architecture, is far from clear-cut. As Robert Beauregard states, "All sites exist first as places."[2] He distinguishes sites from places to separate the construct architects and urban designers create, a site, from the thing we understand through experience, a place. There is no specific process that a place goes through to become a site for design, but this construct is fundamentally important to the generation of architecture. Before the process of design begins, information about the place is gathered. "Gathering" is a misnomer, however. Instead of collecting evidence like a detective to support a hypothesis, you take in all that there *is*, and today this is made even more complicated with the additional virtual layering of the digital world. All that there *is* is then reduced to the "pertinent" information that supports a design idea. The process of analyzing a site and then representing that analysis is, in itself, a design.

A representation of a site only presents a small fragment of a larger understanding about what a site is, what it means. Much like Jorge Luis Borges's "On Exactitude in Science,"[3] where mapmakers in an attempt to construct an accurate representation create a map the size of the country they were mapping, ultimate accuracy ultimately means we will re-create our surroundings. Representations are a filter: they reduce the totality of any given context in order to perceive something transcendent, something that gives meaning beyond the information itself. Methodologically, however, site analysis has traditionally been thought of as an "inventory". Kevin Lynch and Gary Hack, in their introduction to *Site Planning*, refer to this inventory:

> Analysis of the site begins with a personal reconnaissance, which permits a grasp of the essential character of the place and allows the planner to become familiar with its features. Later, then, she can recall mental images of those features as she manipulates them. Analysis proceeds to a more systematic data collection, which may follow some standard list, but lists are treacherous…. Through her analysis, the designer looks for patterns and essences to guide her plan, as well as simply for facts that she must take into account. She ends with a graphic summary, which communicates the fundamental character of the place, as well as how it will most likely respond to the proposed intervention.[4]

Lynch and Hack warn of the "treachery" lurking in the objective authority in lists that are at once systematic data (read: objective) and personal reconnaissance (read: subjective). The potential exists to misrepresent a place by neglecting some aspect of it, and to create architecture with a flawed relationship to site through this neglect. There is a danger of *getting it wrong*: this can be difficult to grasp in today's world of instantaneous and increasingly complex data processing. But the potential fallibility and the subjectivity in constructing a site through representation frame the process of designing architecture.

When Lynch and Hack rely on the planner to see through facts to "patterns and essences," they are describing a way of thinking, not something that can be solved with the same solution every time like an equation. Robin Evans speaks to this when writing on the act of drawing and its translation to the building:

> transfiguration, transition, transmigration, transfer, transmission, transmogrification, transmutation, transposition, transubstantiation, transcendence, any of which would sit happily over the blind spot between the drawing and its object, because we can never be quite certain, before the event, how things will travel and what will happen to them along the way.[5]

Analyzing/representing the site requires technical skills of representation but also a critical way of seeing—seeing a place, and seeing a path through all of the contextual information to what it may mean for a design. Learning this process is critical to restoring site to its relevance to architecture today.

This book is intended to address some basic methods architects use to translate their perceptions to a representation of the complex conditions that physically and mentally "construe" the site, helping to shape the final design. The overarching intention behind introducing the methods and processes within this book is not to generate a comprehensive inventory of all the representational types that may exist between a site and a piece of architecture, but to carefully consider key groups of representational methods, paired together in each part, seeing the dialogue these produce in relationship to each other and to the case study. The representational types discussed are intentionally idiosyncratic, and are intended to be provocative, not comprehensive. Representational methods that have stood the test of time within the discipline through longevity and ubiquity are deliberately paired with emerging and potentially more experimental methods, not to prove the value of one over the other but to consider their individual strengths and weakness in an open-ended discourse. The book is arranged under four broad themes:

- defining site
- experiencing site
- spatializing site
- systematizing site.

The themes and individual chapters can be viewed in sequence as a kind of point and counterpoint, or considered in isolation, independent of each other. The case studies appended to each theme cover strategic architectural projects, providing a bridge from perception to representation to actual built form. Each study covers a specific architectural work teasing out the architect's distinct and individual process, and their process in relation to the representational methods introduced in each part. The case studies are intended to expand the breadth of each part's theme, but are also intended to demonstrate compelling and insightful contemporary relationships to site.

Part I, "Defining Site," explores how architects begin the process of constructing a "site." Chapter 1, on diagramming, will examine the power of reduction in representation by conceiving a site as a bounded or unbounded system through the work of architect/theorists Simon Unwin and Stan Allen. For both Unwin and Allen, site is fundamental to architecture, and it is also the first act of design. But the nature of that act is radically different: for Unwin site is fundamentally a bounded domain, for Allen the site exists in the relationships between things. This chapter will explore these differences, and how the diagram as a representational process of reduction can clarify the initial move made on a site.

Chapter 2, on the site plan, will explore the representational history of the site plan as the key drawing to identify or construe the site, from the notational standards architects read and recognize, to the less normative and representationally specific. The chapter will examine the work of architects such as Richard

Meier, Daniel Libeskind and Enric Miralles, who use the site plan as an all-inclusive tool in the process of design, for the communication of ideas and as design generator.

Chapter 3 introduces the first case study, examining the development and design of a museum to house an archeological ruin in the city of Cartagena, Spain. The city of Cartagena has sought to uncover its own history, literally digging through its layers to reveal the city underneath so that this history now comingles starkly with its present. The Barrio del Foro Romano at the foot of El Molinete hill encompasses a large archeological excavation of what was once a full city block containing a bath and drinking house in the Roman city of Carthago Novo (New Carthage). This Roman block was buried under centuries of alterations and changes to the landscape above. The boundaries of the site are in flux, existing between historical epochs, and the corresponding case study looks at architects Atxu Amann, Andrés Cánovas and Nicolás Maruri's response to these conditions as the project has grown from decorative fence to outdoor museum and canopy, giving a telling study of defining a site.

Part II focuses on experiencing site. Experiencing a work of architecture is profound and visceral. All of your senses participate in the process, going beyond anything a representation can hope to capture. This part introduces two distinct representational types to convey experience. The first, composite montage (Chapter 4), draws on a technique described by James Corner to create an open-ended representational system. Deliberately borrowing from aspects of collage in the Bauhaus and other composite drawing techniques, composite montage is intended to borrow meaning by literally integrating fragments of images from other sources to convey a composite, multivalent, and open-ended representation of a site.

The second representational type, topography (Chapter 5), covers the rich tradition of drawing the most basic aspect of a site that will affect your experience—the ground. Topography has a long-standing notational history embedded in the technical art of map-making, but topography is also the fundamental measurable aspect of any site to convey experience. Kenneth Frampton speaks of this measuring when describing the history of the site as inscribed: "This inscription, which arises out of 'in-laying' the building into the site, has many levels of significance, for it has a capacity to embody, in built form, the prehistory of the place, its archeological past and its subsequent cultivation and transformation across time."[6] Some topography may be easily seen—on hillsides, valleys, cliffs and edges—but the subtler topography in what may seem a flat landscape can be more powerfully affecting than any mountain range. Topography also reveals the trace of drainage, providing an instrumental, pragmatic and poetic understanding of site. This chapter will examine sites and architecture at both ranges of topography, and the link between the technical method of the drawing and the reality of a site.

Architecture is intended to be experienced—it is a fundamental and defining quality of built work. The case study for this part (Chapter 6) is a residential design–build project entitled White House, situated in the dense oak-forested hills near the Lake of the Ozarks in Missouri. Designer–builder Bruce Johnson's response to the changeable context draws from his experience with the site, in both the design process and in building the project on site using predominately reclaimed materials. The project is also about your experience with it, much like land artist Walter de Maria's work *The Lightning Field*, where you are required to overnight at the installation in order to properly experience the work of art. The intimate interior spaces have a constant and changing interplay with the surrounding forest, and your perception of the house changes with its diurnal and seasonal cycles.

Part III centers on spatializing site. The techniques and case studies introduced in this part become increasingly hybridized between the analysis and the design, where the conceptualization or construing of a site is part and parcel with the design itself. Chapter 7 focuses on the tradition of the figure ground, examining the work of Colin Rowe and Fred Koetter in *Collage City*. Building from these precedents, the chapter will concentrate on how the figure ground is a tool for understanding space. Like the diagram, it is exceptionally reductive in order to convey the complexities of urban space—public and private, solid and void, figure and ground, building and street. Because of its reductive nature, however, the technique can yield dramatically altered results with the subtle manipulation of the aspects included in the black of the figure or the white of the ground.

Comparative analysis is the focus of Chapter 8, comparing the work of Junzo Kuroda, Momoyo Kajima, and Yoshiharu Tsukamoto in *Made in Tokyo*, and Robert Venturi, Denise Scott Brown, and Steven Izenour in *Learning from Las Vegas*. The work of these two groups can be seen as a lineage analyzing urban form through the medium of a specific city. Both books (and architects) carry a strong thesis about the city they are studying, and both are seeking a way of representing their analysis to capture the essence of their thesis. The representations they use rely on comparison through repetition and variation.

The case study for Part III (Chapter 9) will investigate the Photographer's Gallery, located in London, by architects Sheila O'Donnell and John Tuomey. The gallery takes advantage of a previous warehouse structure on the site, slotting into the urban fabric of Soho. While it contains photographic prints, huge picture windows frame the urban context, becoming a part of the gallery spaces. The circulation pulls visitors off the street and brings you immediately back to the street at every level, creating a sophisticated interchange between the photographs exhibited, the new and old structure, and the transforming urban fabric.

Part IV considers systematizing site, perceiving the site as a complex order assembled of relatable parts. The concept of a system for the purposes of this book encompasses everything and anything that persists beyond the boundaries of a site, or that can be tapped into. The representational types explored in this part are from architects that take advantage of the role and significance of the systems on site, how it is drawn and made relevant to the design. This part diverges from the previous three by including several traditional and more emergent systems of representation within each chapter. Chapter 10, on flow, considers the analysis of complex and dynamic forces on a site, from natural forces such as time to the movement and trajectories of people and objects in space. These forces, because of their dynamic nature, are difficult to pin down in the static world of representation, but their impact can be overwhelming and even life threatening. While the natures of these forces are dramatically different, they can be understood representationally as a type. Several techniques will be considered that bridge from analysis to representation to design, including work from architects who holistically consider the impact and representation of flow in all its forms.

Chapter 11, on infrastructural networks, will focus on physical infrastructure that as a system responds to the complex and dynamic forces on a site and are networked within larger systems. These systems often fall under the purview of planners or independent authorities that can be taken for granted by architects when considering a site, but play a vital role in shaping a design. Similar to the forces of flow, there are many representational techniques to convey these systems, but they can also be understood representationally as a type. Several techniques will be considered that bond the representational system in the analysis to the design, and the projects shown in this chapter capitalize on infrastructure, both physically in place and as a system to be deployed, to reconceive and transform the site.

The final case study, in Chapter 12, will consider Trollstigplatået at Troll-stigen, Norway, by Reiulf Ramstad Architects. This building and site exist within the network of the National Tourist Routes, which were instigated by the govern-ment to make the natural and cultural attractions of the area more accessible to visitors while also showcasing the country's contemporary design. The site is on the edge of a large glacial valley where a waterfall cascades off the cliffs. Only open during summer months, the design is forced to work within the often opposing systems created by the fluctuating crowds and spring snowmelt. The building is as much about the procession into the landscape from the highway as it is about its own physical presence within the natural and built systems in place, providing a fitting investigation into the forces and infrastructural networks that play a role in constructing the project.

Finally, the Afterword will consider in broad terms how site, as its own arena within the discipline of architecture, continues to expand. Intersections, overlaps, hybridizations and emerging trajectories can now be seen between landscape architecture, land art, infrastructure, sustainability, ecology and architecture. While the book is fundamentally about the architecture's relationship to site, the disciplines and fields that consider or construe the site have grown increasingly nebulous. This final chapter is intended to address and reflect on some of the challenges faced by the role of the representation in what can be seen as a blurring field, and the potential opportunities that can be seen through this transformation.

Notes

1   Hani Rashid and Lise Anne Couture, *Asymptote: Architecture at the Interval* (New York: Rizzoli International Publications and Asymptote Architecture, 1995), 18.

2   Robert Beauregard, "From Place to Site: Negotiating Narrative Complexity," in *Site Matters: Design Concepts, Histories, and Strategies*, ed. Carol J. Burns and Andrea Kahn (New York: Routledge, 2005), 39.

3   Jorge Luis Borges, "On Exactitude in Science," in *Collected Fictions*, trans. Andrew Hurley (New York: Penguin, 1999), 325.

4   Kevin Lynch and Gary Hack, *Site Planning*, 3rd edition (Cambridge, MA: MIT Press, 1984), 7.

5   Robin Evans, "Translations from Drawing to Building," in his *Translations from Drawing to Building and Other Essays* (London: Architectural Association Publications, 1997), 182.

6   Kenneth Frampton, "Towards a Critical Regionalism: Six Points for an Architecture of Resistance," in *The Anti-Aesthetic: Essays on Postmodern Culture*, ed. Hal Foster (Port Townsend, WA: Bay Press, 1983), 26.

Part I

Defining Site

Defining the site is the first architectural act. It may or may not be physical, but it requires action to define what a site is. This definition is significant for both pragmatic and conceptual reasons: something must be designed prior to conceiving of a building that can aid in understanding both functionally and conceptually the rationale for the building's location. Places exist prior to (and after) site (this concept is elaborated on in by Robert Beauregard in his "From Place to Site," listed in the bibliography). Places exist all around us, and are defined by our shared experience in them. You meet at a coffee house, you walk through a canyon, you visit the Eiffel Tower: these are all examples of places, and can be built or natural, designed or merely occupied. A place can be written about, photographed, discussed, walked through, and inhabited; it can be relatively well defined, but can also exist in comparable ambiguity. Site is distinct from this idea of place, because a site is a construct. It is what architects create, within which a design takes shape. The terms "place" and "site" are often used interchangeably by architects and in writings about architecture without intentionally being ambiguous, but this distinction is critical. The definition of a site is the beginning of a design. It is constructed in the mind of a designer, and must be used to communicate the framework within which an architect will operate.

.

1

Diagram

Diagrams are used everywhere in our daily life as a visual aid: in instruction manuals, for life safety, and for way-finding, to name a few. They help visually communicate the unfamiliar in a concise and elementary way. The diagram is, in its broadest sense, a representational tool used to reduce complexity to essential components and communicate critical relationships or tasks. But how does this relate to defining a site? Mark Garcia, in *The Diagrams of Architecture*, defines the diagram as it relates to architecture as "a spatialisation of a selective abstraction and/or reduction of a concept or phenomena. In other words, a diagram is the architecture of an idea or entity."[1] His definition applies a broad understanding of the diagram as a representational tool to architecture as a specific selective and reductive process that occurs in the mind. Defining a site is also essentially a process of reduction that occurs in the mind: it distinguishes the surroundings from everything there is. This reductive process is also highly selective, reducing the surroundings to what an architect determines are its essential components, and this is where the diagram becomes a critical tool.

Simon Unwin, in his book *Analysing Architecture*, describes the first architectural act as "The place where the mind touches the world."[2] It is, for him, an inherently human thing (in the Cartesian sense) to take in your surroundings, as well as the initial conceptualization of architecture. Unwin goes further in *Analysing Architecture* to outline his description of the basic elements of architecture—essentially building blocks from which all architecture derives. As with Garcia's definition of the diagram, Unwin creates a spatialization of a selective abstraction. Like a Lego set, these building blocks are an abstraction of future construction. Intriguingly, Unwin begins with the ground, and the ground frames each of the basic elements:

Diagram

11

The definition of an area of ground is fundamental to the identification of many if not most types of place. It may be no more than a clearing in the forest or it may be a pitch laid out for a football game. It may be small or stretch to the horizon. It need not be rectangular in shape nor need it be level. It need not have a precise boundary but may, at its edges, blend into the surroundings.[3]

Because he begins with the ground, Unwin's elements can also be a way of defining the site. For instance, the "area of ground" diagram shown in Figure 1.1 is both a building block and the more metaphysical locating of a site. It is a rectangle placed in perspective, in relationship to a horizon. The diagram conveys a site that is bounded, and within that boundary contains everything necessary to create architecture. In his "platform" diagram (Figure 1.2), Unwin then extrudes the defined area of ground, so that it is still inscribed by the initial rectangle in relationship to the horizon, but this area now has a form. In the "pit" diagram (Figure 1.3), Unwin reverses the extrusion of the defined area of ground to show a void. Again, the horizon is kept, as well as the initial rectangle, but through its absence the void creates a form again defined by the ground. His "roof" diagram (Figure 1.4) repeats this idea once again: it relies on the same horizon and the defined area, but the rectangle has now lifted off the ground to imply the area beneath.

In all cases, these diagrams depend on our perception of the horizon and perspective within the diagrams to literally "ground" the object described against the background. All of Unwin's basic elements maintain a connection to this imaginary ground that exists somewhere between the foreground and the horizon. Unwin's descriptions for each element of architecture are deliberately open-ended to allow for the greatest variation for potential architecture built from these elements. His diagrams are, on the other hand, measured and concise. They seek to visualize the smallest amount of information necessary to convey the idea. You can imagine that the defined area of ground could be a rectangle,

1.1
[Left] Defined area of ground. Simon Unwin, 1997.

1.2
[Right] Raised area, or platform. Simon Unwin, 1997.

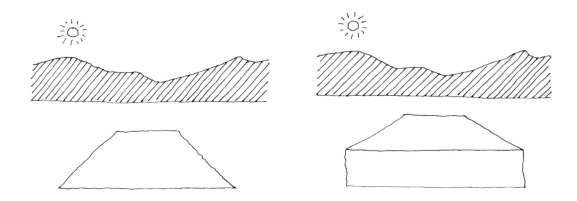

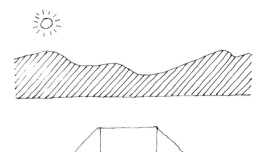

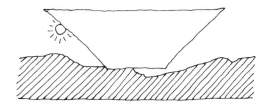

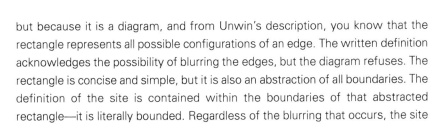

but because it is a diagram, and from Unwin's description, you know that the rectangle represents all possible configurations of an edge. The written definition acknowledges the possibility of blurring the edges, but the diagram refuses. The rectangle is concise and simple, but it is also an abstraction of all boundaries. The definition of the site is contained within the boundaries of that abstracted rectangle—it is literally bounded. Regardless of the blurring that occurs, the site has edges.

Stan Allen, in *Points + Lines: Diagrams and Projects for the City*, seeks "an architecture that leaves space for the uncertainty of the real."[4] Like Unwin, Allen is seeking to define (or redefine) architecture: how we go about it, and what *it* is. Allen uses the city to define the parameters around which architecture can happen, distinct from a more abstract notion of ground. Borrowing a concept from the physical sciences called "field conditions," which is used to understand the complex, changeable and dynamic forces only seen by their effects, he creates a definition of site that exists without edges. For Allen:

> a field condition could be any formal or spatial matrix capable of unifying diverse elements while respecting the identity of each. Field configurations are loosely bound aggregates characterized by porosity and local interconnectivity ... Form matters, but not so much the forms of things but the forms *between* things.[5]

To illustrate what a field condition is, Allen avoids a concise diagram to literally inscribe varying notions of edge. Instead, he resorts to a series of diagrams to provide examples of what field conditions are (Figure 1.5). When examining this matrix, there are distinct commonalities: each show a clustering of black shapes that read together, in part by an implied boundary, but also because they form a kind of pattern. There is also a sense of balance, a kind of gestalt, between the amount of white and the amount of black in each diagram, where the black objects compete with the white figure formed by the black objects. The site is

1.3
[Left] Lowered area, or pit. Simon Unwin, 1997.

1.4
[Right] Roof, or canopy. Simon Unwin, 1997.

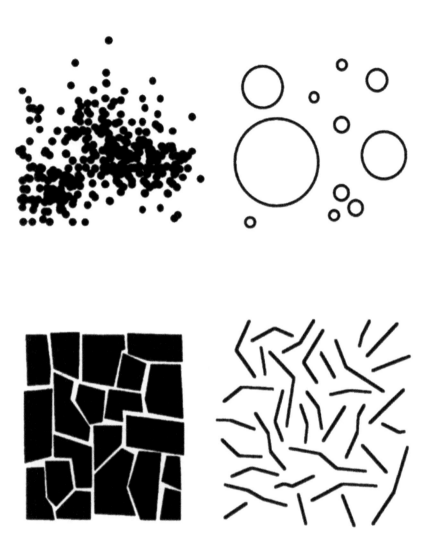

essentially defined by recognizing the pattern or the field condition in the surroundings; its limits are set by the emergence of the pattern, not by a containing boundary. For Allen, it is the relationships between things not the things themselves that define the site.

Both Unwin's and Allen's conceptualizations are equally effective and powerful definitions of a site: one set of diagrams should not be privileged over the other. They both seek to conceptualize architecture through site and by diagramming. Robert E. Somol, in his introduction to Peter Eisenman's *Diagram Diaries*, discusses the nature of the diagram: "unlike drawing or text, *partis pris* or bubble notation—it appears in the first instance to operate precisely between form and word ... it is a performative rather than a representational device ... it is a tool of the virtual rather than the real."[6] The performative nature Somol describes is the key to understanding why diagramming should be considered when defining the site. The diagram should perform: it is a device that acts between things and words. Like Unwin's sentiment that "architecture is where the mind touches the world,"[7] the diagram is active as a tool of the virtual (outside the real). The author can select what to abstract and then abstract it, but the diagram has the power to communicate something about what it represents, as well as the power to change the way the author thinks. The performative nature to the diagram can be seen in the way both authors rely on written descriptions to clarify their diagrams. The diagram, without explanation, could represent many things to someone viewing it. Their descriptions allow for your perception to be shifted to see what they intend you to see. For both authors, the diagrams also clarify the idea behind the diagram, allowing the possibility that the authors learned something by generating it.

The definition of the site is fundamental to what you may define as architecture; it is the first act of design, and it frames all future design decisions. But the nature of that frame can be radically different: for Unwin, site is fundamentally a bounded domain; for Allen, the site exists in an unbounded state, at the scale where the field conditions of the site are made evident. These two ways of thinking through diagrams are a useful comparison, because they offer, in some sense, the two poles at which a site can be defined. In school, and as a professional, it can be deceptive to equate the definition of the site with the property boundaries—it represents the "owned" zone, but it rarely represents what is buildable or architecturally compelling or appropriate. A diagram, based solely on the property lines (Figure 1.6), can look similar to Unwin's definition of the area of ground (without the essential perspectival projection). Like Unwin's diagram, it offers a limit to the surroundings so that within those restraints, you can develop a refined understanding of the physical forces and attributes of that bounded domain.

Other forces are at work, though, that can push back or run entirely counter to these boundaries that will aid in defining of the site and further delimit what may be built. Zoning setbacks and regulations put in place by city or town planners, often for health and safety reasons, are a case in point for this kind of delimiting force. For example, the rampant vertical expansion spurred by the technological invention of the skyscraper has helped shape the urban fabric we

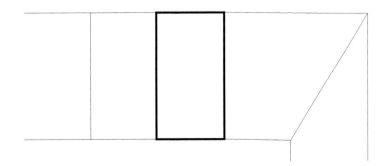

1.6
Site diagram using lot lines to demarcate boundaries.

Diagram 15

recognize in any metropolis. Because of the size of the buildings being built, there were dramatic consequences on the life on the street, where daylight became scarce and wind tunnel effects were common. In response to this, New York City instigated a series of vertical setback requirements that would help allow daylight to reach the streets (Figure 1.7). Because developers were interested in maxi-

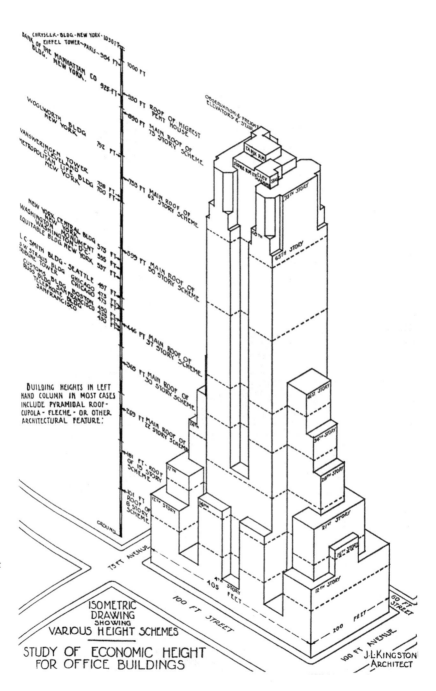

1.7
Study of economic height for office buildings. W.C. Clark, *Skyscraper: A Study in the Economic Height of Modern Office Buildings* (New York and Cleveland: American Institute of Steel Construction, inc., 1930), 15.

mizing their square footage, the setback requirements became the architectural expression of the building, made infamous by the renderings done by Hugh Ferriss.[8] This sophisticated diagram showing economic height illustrates a kind of three-dimensional boundary for a site—it shows the extents to which one could build, and reflects the architecture produced within its restrictions.

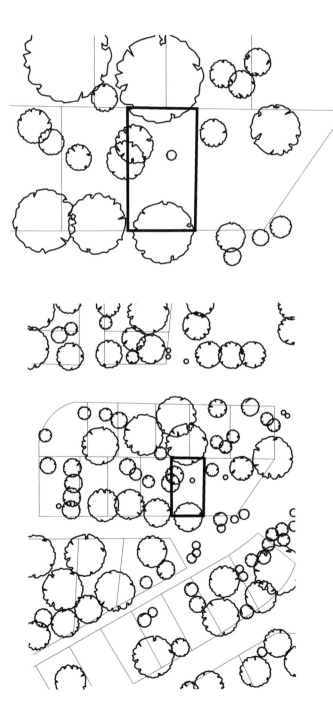

1.8
Site diagram at the scale that shows the trees on and adjacent to a given property.

1.9
Site diagram at the scale that shows how the trees reveal the blocks of the neighborhood.

Diagram

17

Other forces that will define the site do not serve as boundaries, but dictate larger patterns that are omnipresent at specific scales. For instance, consider the trees present within the boundaries of a hypothetical piece of property (Figure 1.8). No discernible pattern can be seen at the scale of the bounded site. However, if the scale is altered to consider a larger area (Figure 1.9), the field condition or what might be called a "grain" to the site emerges. We can now see the figure of the voids read against the trees. Not unlike Ray and Charles Eames's *Powers of Ten*, structure emerges out of noise as the scale shifts.[9]

At an even greater scale (Figure 1.10), a different grain emerges on this hypothetical neighborhood, showing how the patterns of streets and buildings

1.10
Site diagram at the scale that shows the grain of the buildings and the impact of a stream cutting through the gridded streets.

Defining Site

have shifted against the underlying stream that has resisted the imposition of a Cartesian grid. Both of these field conditions are critical to the definition of the site, for pragmatic and poetic reasons. Zooming back in to the scale of the single lot (Figure 1.11), the streambed is again unrecognizable. Without acknowledging the presence of the stream as part of the site, it becomes easy to neglect its impact or its worth.

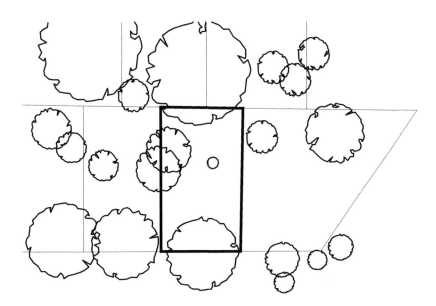

Diagramming is invaluable for demonstrating the potential of a site, and it can also be a design tool. Rem Koolhaas and the Office of Metropolitan Architecture's proposal for the Parc de la Villette (Figure 1.12) demonstrates an intriguing precedent where the definition of the site and the proposal for that site are distinctly intertwined. The proposal employs both a bounded and unbounded approach to defining the site. The defined area of ground can be seen on the diagram "Initial hypothesis," where the outer boundary of the park is delineated, divided by the canal and two largest existing buildings. This is the boundary of all that will be designed within that space, and the size of the program is broken into three hatched areas and overlaid on the diagram of the site.

Koolhaas was interested in creating "a 'method' that combines architectural specificity with programmatic indeterminacy … The essence of the competition becomes, therefore, how to orchestrate on a metropolitan field the most dynamic coexistence of x, y, and z activities."[10] Because the park would accommodate an enormous variety of activity that would change over time, he needed a method to define the parameters of that activity. The bands seen in "The strips" Koolhaas describes as "the first primordial gesture [on] the whole site."[11] These bands demarcate zones of potential in the site; each diagram analyzes distinct field

Diagram

1.12
Site diagrams, Office of
Metropolitan
Architecture/Rem
Koolhaas, Parc de la
Villette Competition
Proposal, Paris, France,
1983.

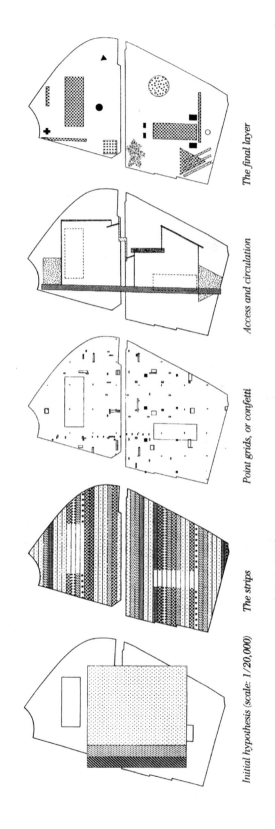

The final layer

Access and circulation

Point grids, or confetti

The strips

Initial hypothesis (scale: 1/20,000)

conditions present or imagined within the larger site of the Parc de la Villette. By layering these diagrams, the final proposal maintains the essence of the original banding within the boundary of the site, becoming a complex tapestry of specific built and landscaped moments that will engender the activities conceived with the original banding.

The diagram is a representational process of reduction that will also clarify the initial move made on a site. As with the method Koolhaas generates for the Parc de la Villette, it will reduce the components of a site to what will directly contribute to the form. Those components can inscribe distinct edges to work around, or establish larger patterns in the environment that cannot be overlooked. Architecture is not simply a process of elimination based on limitations set in place by the definition of the site. Defining the site will allow you, as the designer, to understand what choices can be made, and begin to structure the factors that will impact larger moves made to the site and predict the consequences of any move that runs against or bends away from what already exists.

Notes

1   Mark Garcia, "Introduction: Histories and Theories of the Diagrams of Architecture," in *The Diagrams of Architecture: A Reader*, ed. Mark Garcia (Chichester: John Wiley & Sons, 2010), 18.

2   Simon Unwin, *Analysing Architecture*, 3rd edition (New York: Routledge, 2009), 32.

3   Unwin, *Analysing Architecture*, 37.

4   Stan Allen, *Points + Lines: Diagrams and Projects for the City* (New York: Princeton Architectural Press, 1999), 102.

5   Allen, *Points + Lines*, 92.

6   Robert E. Somol, "Dummy Text, or The Diagrammatic Basis of Contemporary Architecture," in *Diagram Diaries*, by Peter Eisenman (New York: Universe Publishing, 1999), 8.

7   Unwin, *Analysing Architecture*, 32.

8   For more on this topic, see Hugh Ferriss, *Power in Buildings: An Artist's View of Contemporary Architecture* (Santa Monica, CA: Hennessey + Ingalls, 1998), 48–51.

9   *Powers of Ten*, documentary short film, directed and written by Charles and Ray Eames (1968; DVD: Chatsworth, CA: Image Entertainment, 2000).

10   Rem Koolhaas, *OMA–Rem Koolhaas: Architecture, 1970–1990*, ed. James Lucan, trans. David Block (New York: Princeton Architectural Press, 1991), 86.

11   Koolhaas, *OMA–Rem Koolhaas*, 86.

Diagram   **21**

2

The Site Plan

Architecture is conveyed through representation. Distinct from the visual arts, the medium of architecture exists between the actual object being designed and the mind of the designer.[1] We also design through representations. These representations act as a notational system, similar to a composed score for a piece of music, which makes the definition of "representation" in architecture complicated: it is both a likeness of something, and a "set of instructions" to create something else.[2] You do not literally *see* the sounds of music on a score; instead, a notational system allows you to coordinate between other players, the conductor, and the composer to arrive at a cohesive whole. You agree that the sound of "A" is all the same pitch, and you agree "A" is located in the same place according to clef, and if the score is correctly written and you all agree to the same tempo, music (instead of noise) will emerge through the act of playing. Representation in architecture is made of similar notational conventions and origin points. Like the staff of a score, parallel projection is the basic translational armature that plans, sections, elevations and axonometric drawing all use. Parallel projection is a drawing device that removes any distortion the eye sees in perspective (which permits us to understand depth in space). The technique of parallel projection then creates a drawing that can be measured; its dimensions, through the process of scale, will translate to actual object dimensions. From this basic key, the entire foundation of architectural drawing emerges, which will be used to communicate the future building to contractors and clients through an entirely separate medium from its construction materials.

The site plan lies at the intersection of architecture's notational conventions and the individual architect's definition of the site. Like a musical composition, this drawing can function as set of instructions for the architect's vision to those who will actually build the site and architecture, but it also functions as a transla-tional tool to communicate the architectural idea and its relationship to the site to a client or to the public. Because of this dual role, it is deceptive to think of the site plan as a likeness of the building on the site *or* a mere set of instructions to a contractor. The site plan is the locale for establishing and defining the parameters of the site in clear connection to the future piece of architecture, and it is often ambiguously a likeness of the architecture and site as well as the notation for architectural intent (not necessarily for the purpose of construction). Because this ambiguity is in the control of the individual architect, site plans are drawn in many ways, but can be roughly divided into those who use the drawing of the site plan to reveal a specific and intended relationship to a site and those who use the site plan as the design milieu for the emerging architecture.

Richard Meier's site plan for the Smith House (Figure 2.1) is a quintessential example that exposes the architect's intention towards the site and its relationship to the house designed. The outlines of rocks and foliage have been very deliberately drawn whereas the neighboring houses are entirely excluded from the plan to reinforce the house's connection to the landscape. Meier chose to indicate the topography of the land's steep descent as well as the roof of the project—this immediately draws our eye to the transition from the naturally undulating lines of the slope to the orthogonal lines that form the plinth on which the house sits. In its built form, the plinth is a soft green lawn in front of the house, without the crisply articulated mass the drawing conveys. In the representation, the formal geometry of the house is negotiated through the lines of the topography before it is articulated in the roof elevation. The white space of the site plan is also intentionally ambiguous, so that the lines and textures notating the site provide strictly as much information as is necessary to deliberately construct the transition from the wilder, less kempt natural setting, and the orderly, more structured geometry of the house. For example, at the base of the hill an orthogonal corner demarcates the upper left edge of the drawing. Its incompleteness provides just enough information to convey an extension of the landscape beyond the drawing, while remaining unclear what this portion of a rectangle is in the drawing (in reality it is a crumbling stone jetty). The white space beyond the rocks implies the sea, but illustrating waves or the depth of the ocean is unimportant in the site plan. The sea is left white to reinforce the view beyond the rocks.

Providing only the essential sense of the site is an often-repeated technique in a site plan. It does not mean that the architect has neglected aspects that are beyond the edges of the site or in the white space of the drawing. These details are not important to conveying the architecture's relationship to the site. Renzo Piano's site plan for the Otranto Urban Regeneration Workshop (Figure 2.2) in Italy is another key example of limiting the scope of the site to best reveal the architecture's relationship to it. The site is indicated in the plan as bold black lines that hug three edges of the drawing, outlining a square or piazza. Dashed lines reflect the conjoined buildings that act as solid mass. The square appears intimate

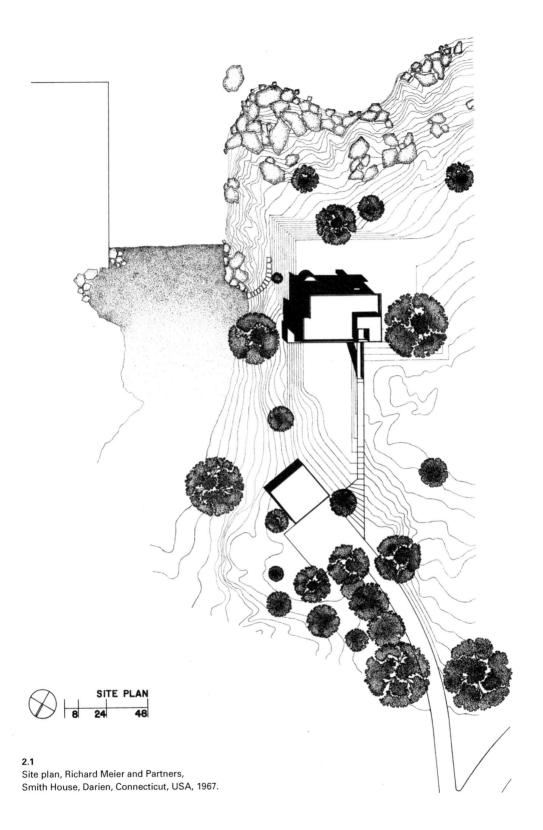

SITE PLAN

| 8 | 24 | 48 |

2.1
Site plan, Richard Meier and Partners,
Smith House, Darien, Connecticut, USA, 1967.

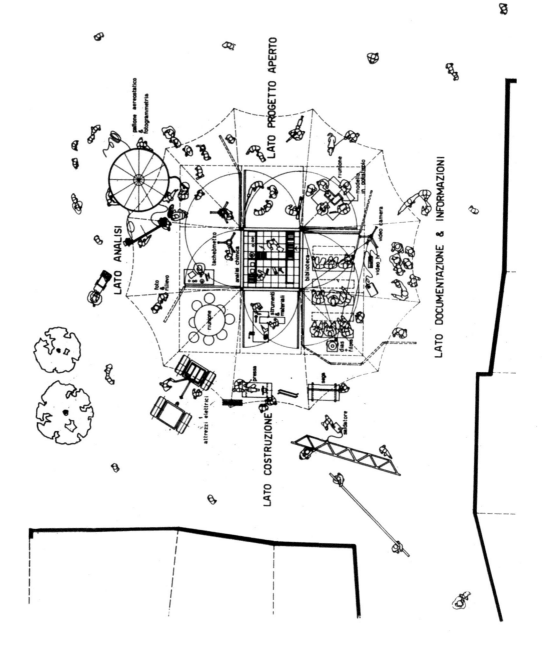

because of the implied scale: the ground plan is shown (as opposed to the roof), and the entourage of people seen aerially are visibly engaged in the process of unfolding the workshop architecture on the ground. The project was commissioned through UNESCO to aid in the rehabilitation of historic centers, and Otranto was chosen as a demonstration and initial experiment. The architecture of the workshop was essentially a cube that would be delivered and installed in an urban square, acting as a base of operations for the duration of the work so that residents would not be moved out of their homes. The site for this project was absolutely critical to the program, but the reason to illustrate the surroundings in the barest means was in part because of the mobility of the architecture. The workshop was intended to travel to historic centers, and while the purpose of the structure was to preserve the surrounding architecture, its structure did not need to respond to the architectural context because it was temporary. The site needed to address the scale of these urban centers, so only the representation of the square at ground level is present in Piano's plan.

Not all architects define the same site in a similar manner. The easiest way to understand this is by looking at competition entries for a given site, in part because every drawing in a competition entry is critical and must help to explain

2.3
Site plan, Steven Holl Architects, Helsinki Contemporary Art Museum competition proposal, Helsinki, Finland, 1992.

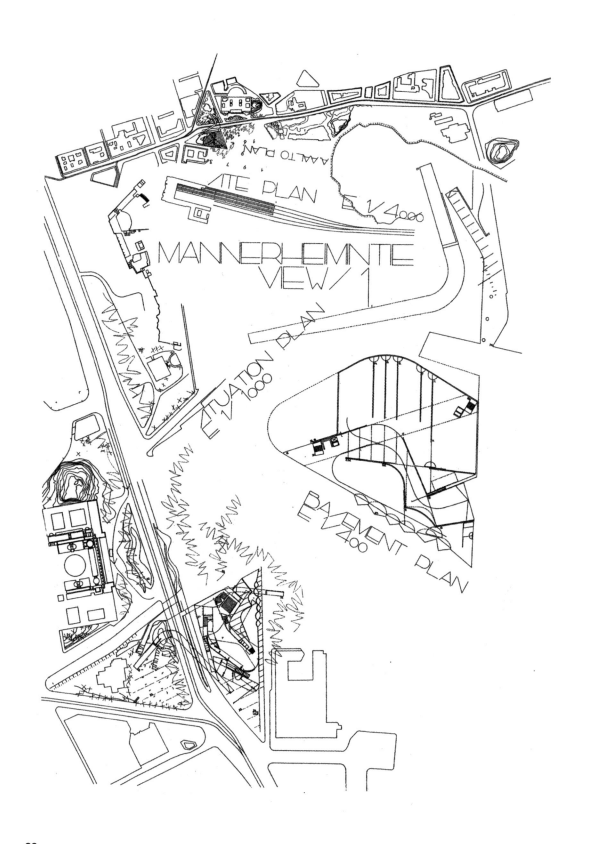

SITE PLAN 1/4000

AALTO PLAN

MANNERHEIMINTIE
VIEW/1

SITUATION PLAN 1/1000

BASEMENT PLAN 1/200

Defining Site

the larger design concept. For instance, in 1992 an invited competition was run for the Helsinki Contemporary Art Museum in Finland. One entrant was Steven Holl, an architect known for his vigorously figural buildings. In the site plan for the competition (Figure 2.3), Steven Holl chose to indicate the urban fabric—the "grain" or field condition—with solid masses. This kind of site plan is not uncommon for Holl: he often uses a figure ground to draw attention to the figure that runs counter to the predominant grain.[3] The scale of this site plan is quite large, and the museum plugs a perceived hole in the urban fabric by introducing a mass to what would be a void in his drawing that reinforces the edges of the street.

Enric Miralles and Carmen Pinos, entrants in the same competition, also had a specific graphic approach that reinforces their larger architectural ideas through the pervasive use of lines, often with only a single line weight. Their site plan for the competition was a combination of two different scales, and included a site section and basement plan (Figure 2.4). The need for so many drawings in a single image becomes clear by tracing the paths of these lines: the property given for this competition lies at the intersection of two major boulevards and a train station. There is also a body of water, Töölö Bay, outlined, which is indicated in Holl's site plan as two large organic grey shapes. The introduction of multiple scales in the drawing illuminates the tiers of movement on the site. The basement plan connects the movement of the site to the architecture, showing how the loading and parking are integrated into the building as well as the larger trajectories of the city circulation. The architect's intent can be seen through the specific choices in representational technique, but it is also possible to see how the choice of representation for the drawing steered the architects to their final design.

Neil M. Denari's work is renowned for pushing the envelope of representational techniques, and he was at the forefront of the transition to computer-aided drafting in design. His site plan for the Museum of the 20th Century (Figure 2.5), for example, shows a rendered elevation of the roof collaged into an aerial photograph. While employing three-dimensional computer modeling to construct his schemes, Denari also uses the drawing of the site plan to design. In response to this competition, he created "A system of Cartesian pathways of circulation [that] connect ten cloudforms."[4] He chose to place the site for his museum at the Los Angeles International Airport (LAX)—you can see the edge of one airplane on the top of the aerial photograph. The project borrows from the immediate context of highway on- and off-ramps to graft the circulation into a more gridded system in the project. Graft is an appropriate term—he is literally building in entry points to his museum at every edge where his drawing meets the photograph. The photograph also builds in a contextual reference that the drawing cannot: the museum is designed for the twentieth century, and the use of aerial photography came about during this century. There is a factual capturing of the bustle of the airport now frozen in the photograph. It is a privileged view from a plane or

The Site Plan

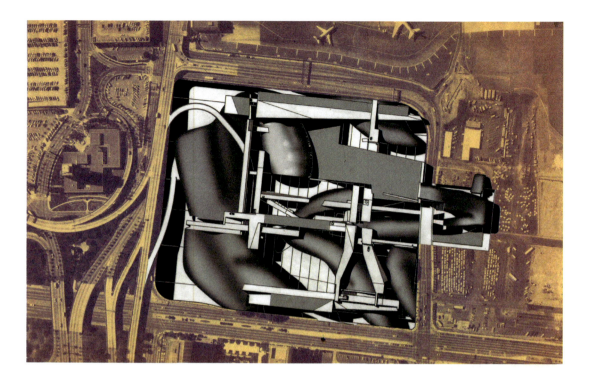

2.5
Site plan, Neil M. Denari
Architects Inc., Museum
of the 20th Century
competition proposal,
Los Angeles, California,
USA, 1993.

2.6
Site plan—layered traces
and shadows, Dagmar
Richter, Earth-scratcher
for Century City
proposal, Los Angeles,
California, USA, 1990.

satellite that we may take for granted with contemporary mapping tools on the Internet, and it is critical to Denari's larger concept for the project. The circulation, from the site and within the project, imagines you are flying through his "cloudforms." By freezing movement with a photograph, the viewer can be persuaded to imagine the site plan as a moment captured in time, and connotes our own sense of movement through the project.

The work of Dagmar Richter goes beyond the referential and connotative, and begins to carve out the architecture from the site by laying down what she refers to as the "traces" of the site in the drawing. Her work is composite in nature. For her proposal for Century City, Richter describes her method as "reading" or "recording" the past to engage the present (Figure 2.6).

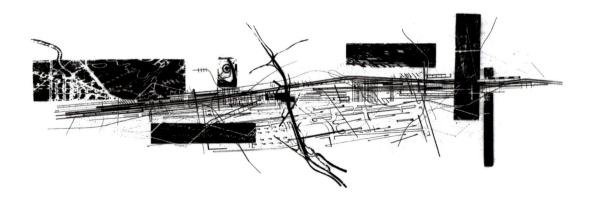

Defining Site

Using historical maps, she draws the traces of the site's past as a collection of film and television studio sets that was transformed into a community of retail, hotels, condominiums, dining, nightlife and business. This became "a new topography of traces that incorporated the previously hidden ones that had been bulldozed by developers."[5] Then the shadows of the contemporary buildings, recorded at different times of day as "an axonometric collapse of the vertical object,"[6] were collected and overlaid on this composite of the historical imagery, along with a "filmic analysis of the site's image" (essentially a photomontage of the façades; see Figure 2.7). The plan of the project elucidates the larger process of revealing the site; the armature for the form she proposes for the city—an Earth-scratcher—"connects two different green spaces through a set of anti-programs and artificial landscapes in the form of numerous lines, surfaces, and volumes that connect, carry, and shelter human activities."[7] The project is effectively the design process of understanding the site.

Daniel Libeskind's work also acts to couple the generation of the site plan with the design process itself. "Re-leasing the View" (Figure 2.8) was part of his original competition entry for the Potsdamer Platz in 1991. The site plan unpacks the history of the site, which is also the formal proposal of the scheme, to become a kind of city in miniature through the history of the Platz. Potsdamer Platz was historically a vital center in Berlin at the intersection of several major streets. The area was devastated at the end of World War II, and when the Berlin Wall was constructed, it literally sliced the Platz in half, one side in the West, the other in the East. When the wall came down, this intersection had become a wasteland, and the competition from which this entry was created was intended to reinvigorate the area. Libeskind's proposal re-envisions the original intersection of the streets that once met on the site, as well as the historical moments that transpired there. These slices of street and times were projected and recombined into the final plan proposal, as well as the site plan. As with Dagmar Richter's Century City proposal, original maps were redrawn, fragmented, and overlaid to create each slice or "puzzle piece."

2.7
Site plan—filmic analysis and axonometric collapse, Dagmar Richter, Earth-scratcher for Century City proposal, Los Angeles, California, USA, 1990.

The Site Plan

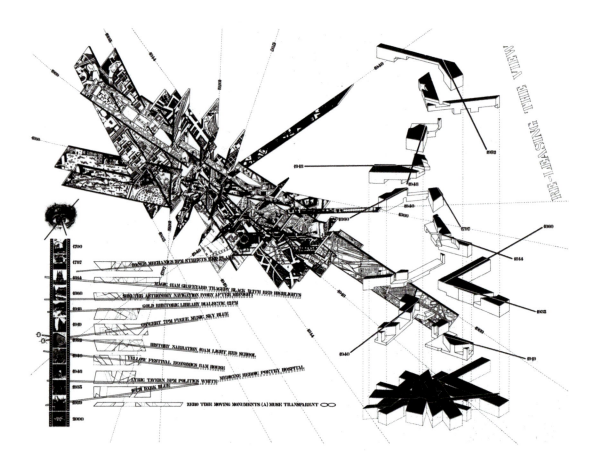

2.8
Site plan, Studio Daniel
Libeskind, Re-leasing the
View competition
proposal, Potsdamer
Platz, Berlin, Germany,
1991.

What can be seen in all of these variations is an overarching awareness of the key features of a site and its impact on the final design. The site plan does not need to be the locale for this discovery, but it can reflect the attitude of its maker. The process of drawing can also have a dramatic effect on the actual architecture, so the work can emerge very literally out of the interpretation of the physical site, as well as the media used. The definition of the site within a site plan is the reflection of the conscious and unconscious intuitions and analysis of the author, allowing the viewer to perceive the design through the author's eyes. In this respect there can be no right or wrong way in which to draw a site plan: it forces the author to draw the site in relationship to the architecture. It is the drawing where we expressly place whatever is designed in a framed context so that both are understood as a whole.

Notes

1   For more on this topic, see Robin Evans, "Translations from Drawing to Building," in his *Translations from Drawing to Building and Other Essays* (London: Architectural Association, 1997), 152–193.

2   Stan Allen, "Mapping the Unmappable: On Notation," in his *Practice: Architecture, Technique and Representation* (Amsterdam: Overseas Publishers Association, 2000), 32.

3   For more examples of Steven Holl's use of the figure ground, see his *Pamphlet Architecture 13: Edge of a City* (New York: Princeton Architectural Press and Pamphlet Architecture, 1991).

4   Neil M. Denari, *Gyroscopic Horizons* (New York: Princeton Architectural Press, 1999), 79.

5   Dagmar Richter, *XYZ: The Architecture of Dagmar Richter* (London: Laurence King Publishing, 2001), 57.

6   Richter, *XYZ*, 57.

7   Richter, *XYZ*, 65.

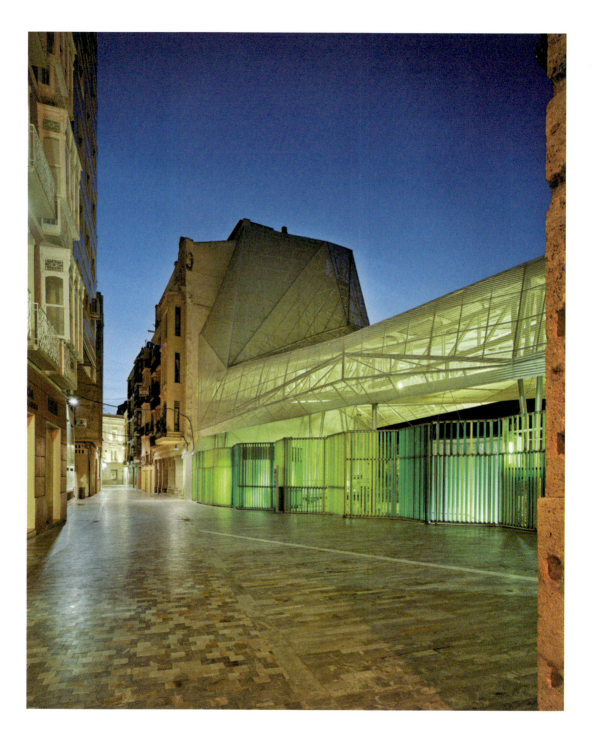

3.1
View from the street,
Amann-Cánovas-Maruri,
El Molinete, Cartagena,
Spain, 2011.

3

Case Study

El Molinete—Cartagena, Spain

Cartagena, as an older European city, has undergone many transformations. From the Carthaginian settlement of Qart Hadast to the Roman city of Carthago Novo, through Arab control in the Middle Ages, to its current Spanish name Cartagena, the culture, fabric of the city, and the buildings themselves have slowly evolved, but its enduring assets establish Cartagena's significance in the history of the region and beyond.

The city is founded on a natural harbor in an area dominated by coastal mountains in what is now the region of Murcia on the Mediterranean Sea (Figure 3.2). These mountains provided defensibility to the harbor, which naturally led to the formation of naval operations that continue today. The hills are also rich with silver, and mining in the surrounding mountains has gone on since the Carthaginians first settled the area. These mineral resources have historically contributed to the prosperity in the region and the continuous transformation of the city since its inception.[1] Today, the city has invested in making that history available to the public by commissioning the design, construction, and preservation of several cultural landmarks. This has instigated a new kind of morphology in the city, where the history is very literally "mined," peeling away the layers of history and built artifacts to reveal the ancient cities underneath.

The Barrio del Foro Romano at the foot of El Molinete Park encompasses a large archeological excavation of what was once a full city block that contained thermal baths, a forum and a domus in the Roman city of Carthago Novo (New Carthage). This Roman block was originally buried under centuries of alterations and changes to the land and city above. The site plan by the Madrid-based architects Amann-Cánovas-Maruri was drawn to reveal the shifting grids of the two cities (Figure 3.3). The Roman city remains stand out in red against the grey-

3.2
Site diagram of
Cartagena, Spain
showing El Molinete Park
relative to the Medieval
fortress walls and traces
of older towns now
incorporated into the city.

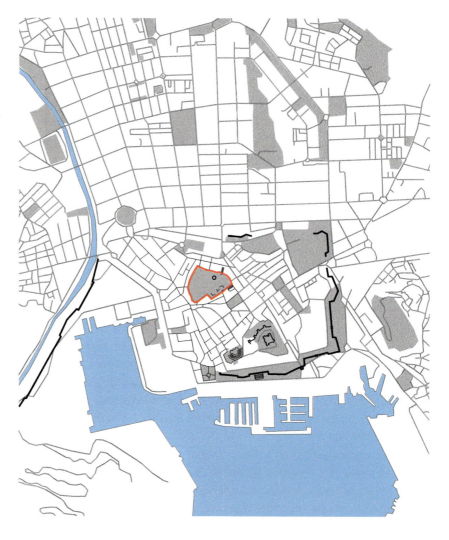

hatched buildings that show the massing of the street today. Amann-Cánovas-Maruri was commissioned by the Cartagena Puerto de Culturas to first design a fence to protect the exposed ruins. This fence helped to re-establish the urban fabric disrupted by the ruins, providing a colorful boundary to denote the older city from the new. After the fence was built, the Cartagena Puerto de Culturas approached the architects again, this time to create a canopy to protect the remains from exposure to ultraviolet rays and precipitation. The canopy and fence were re-envisioned as an outdoor museum that would provide pathways among the ruins and educational information about the remaining uncovered and displayed artifacts, the original Roman city, and how the buildings would have functioned at that time.

The transformation from literal boundary into an outdoor museum places this case study in a unique position relative to defining the site, because the physical site has changed over the progress of the design. When the architects

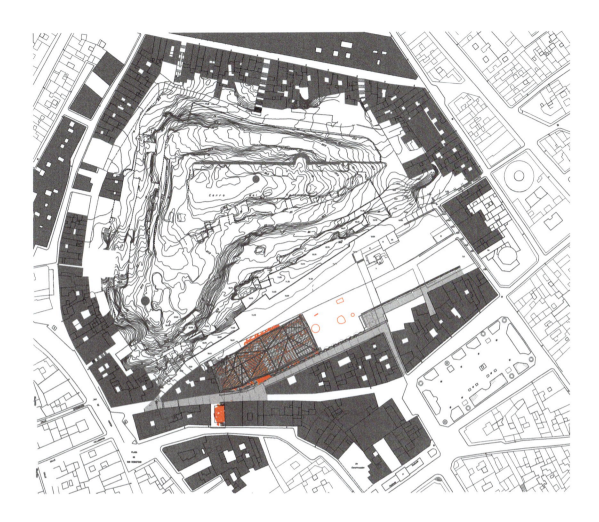

were initially commissioned to create the fence, activating the boundary on the street side was a focus for the overall scheme. The fence was not altered when the transformation to museum took place—it continues to undulate along the sidewalk, and the spacing of the fence façade allows you a glimpse to the ruins below (Figure 3.4). The boundary of the archeological excavation seen in the site plan is also the site for the initial architectural intervention. Spaces for seating and shade trees are carved out of the edge to radically readdress the contemporary city. This reformed edge provides a public space to fold observation back on the urban fabric. Cartagena is now a compelling and eclectic mix of new and old. To pave the way for future construction, many of the older structures in the city have been demolished, but efforts were made to preserve the rich architectural heritage and density at the street by maintaining the façades of older structures. Now many of these façades, held up by scaffolding, await future infill development to support them. The effect within the city is not dissimilar to the

3.3
Site plan,
Amann-Cánovas-Maruri,
El Molinete, Cartagena,
Spain, 2011.

3.4
View of the fence edge,
Amann-Cánovas-Maruri,
El Molinete, Cartagena,
Spain, 2011.

fence of the Barrio del Foro Romano—the façades act to define the public space, while providing glimpses to a radically changed context behind them. When viewing the museum from the top of El Molinete Park, the character of this bounded urban space as a porous membrane can be easily seen (Figure 3.5).

Defining Site

The new canopy that hovers over the Barrio del Foro Romano effectively encapsulates the excavation while remaining open and visually attached to the larger archeological park of El Molinete. Architect Atxu Amann describes this effect: "The intervention unifies all the remains in a single space, allowing a continuous perception of the whole site. It's a transition element between very different city conditions, in size and structure, from the dense city centre to the sloping park."[2]

3.5
View from El Molinete Archeological Park, Amann-Cánovas-Maruri, El Molinete, Cartagena, Spain, 2011.

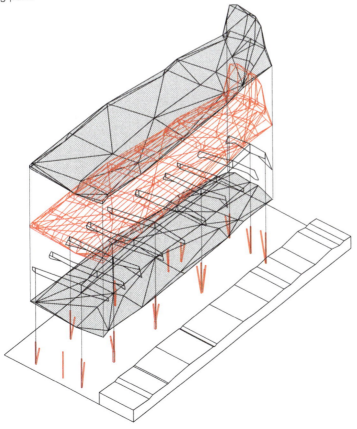

3.6
Exploded axonometric, Amann-Cánovas-Maruri, El Molinete, Cartagena, Spain, 2011.

The roof is constructed of a 74-meter-long steel lattice (about the width of a soccer field) held up by a series of bundled columns that range in height. Three principal longitudinal trusses span between the columns allowing the canopy to appear to float over the existing ruins, extending up to eleven meters in cantilever.[3] A network of steel members ties together the principal longitudinal trusses to create the effect of a lattice and make the entire three-dimensional surface work as a whole to distribute the forces. The roof is also an extension of the hillside: as conceived in the architects' initial rendering, the actual digital representation of the hill carries over into the faceted landscape of the roof to perceptually re-cover the excavation, essentially reburying the exposed artifacts (Figure 3.7). The surface of the roof then peels up the party wall of the adjacent building to mitigate the transition from the park slope to the built fabric and the street.

The canopy is supported on a matrix of only thirteen eccentrically placed and bundled columns—the plan of the project reveals the dramatically minimal intervention at the ground level (Figure 3.8). The columns step lightly through the ruins; each one branches to become an inverted tripod, allowing the columns to read as lightweight structural members while also assisting with the asymmetrical load distribution. These bundled columns also serve as water drainage from the canopy. While delicately emerging out of the ruins, the foundation supports of each column extend into the ground by twenty meters to

3.7
Conceptual rendering, Amann-Cánovas-Maruri, El Molinete, Cartagena, Spain, 2011.

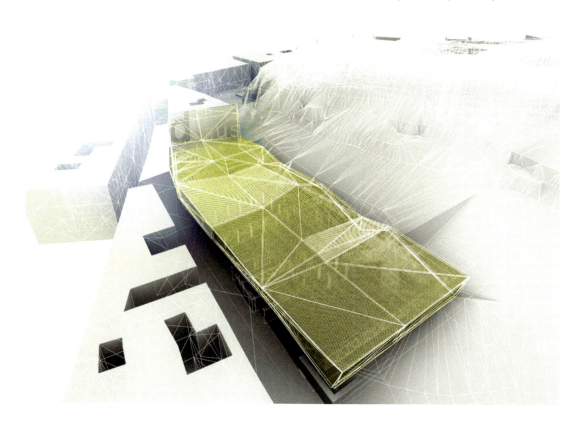

Defining Site

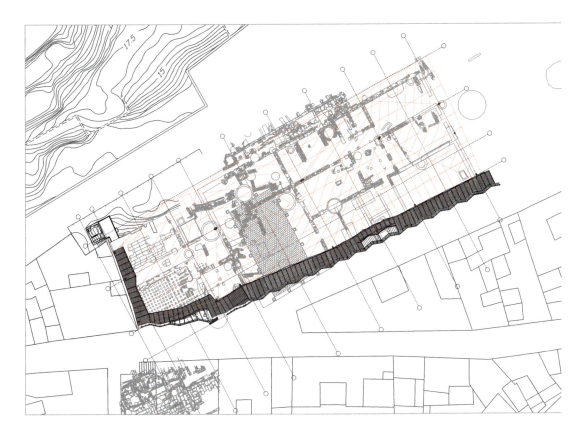

accommodate regional seismic loading.[4] The canopy is an undulating surface, reinforcing the action of the fence in plan, while sitting well enough above it to feel related but deliberately unattached, so that, like the openings in the fence, the separation invites you to peek through the gap created. The shading the canopy provides is created using a lightweight modular system of corrugated multiwall translucent polycarbonate sheets in combination with perforated steel plates.[5] This modular system reflects the original rendering of the building and continues to reinforce the translation of the topography to faceted landscape.

Inside the enclosure, the green and yellow polycarbonate strips of the fence cast a glow on the ruins, making the new read simultaneously with the old. In the same manner that the neighboring building façades work to enliven the streets, the fence plays as both colorful framework and participant to the scene underneath the canopy. Each structure operates entirely independently of the aesthetics that the Roman ruins or the adjacent buildings offer, without trying to subvert or undermine the value of the surrounding older structures. The pathways within the enclosure also offer a neutralizing force that works between the fence and existing ruins to navigate the drop in level (and in time) from the current street level to the Roman city street level. Made of wood decking, the pathways are distinct from the stone paving of the adjacent street and the predominately stone ruins, as if they could be removed. The route is curatorial (Figure 3.10)—as it

3.8
Plan of the ruins, Amann-Cánovas-Maruri, El Molinete, Cartagena, Spain, 2011.

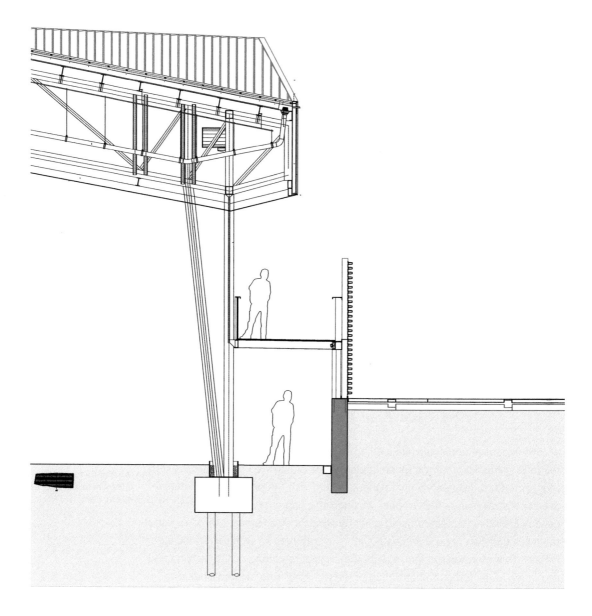

3.9
Detailed section,
Amann-Cánovas-Maruri,
El Molinete, Cartagena,
Spain, 2011.

takes you down through time to the level of the ruins, it also delivers you to the artifacts that have been left, like the close range view of the column capitals in the ruins.

The roof plan (Figure 3.11) reiterates the site plan at a more detailed scale. The canopy is seen in elevation while illuminating the ruins below; the plan is a kind of X-ray view through the site and through time. The drawing is cut high into the hillside, showing part of the terrain of El Molinete as an abstract topography, also capturing part of the existing urban fabric to show the complex clustering of the surrounding buildings and texture of the stone-paved streets. The drawing exposes the almost contradictory nature of the project: its materiality is entirely

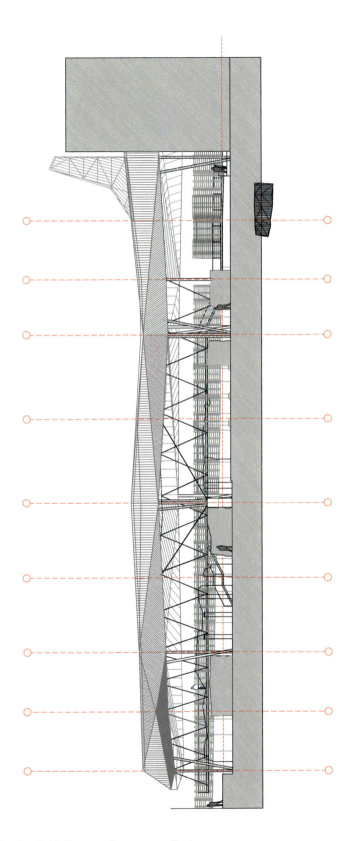

3.10
Section,
Amann-Cánovas-Maruri,
El Molinete, Cartagena,
Spain, 2011.

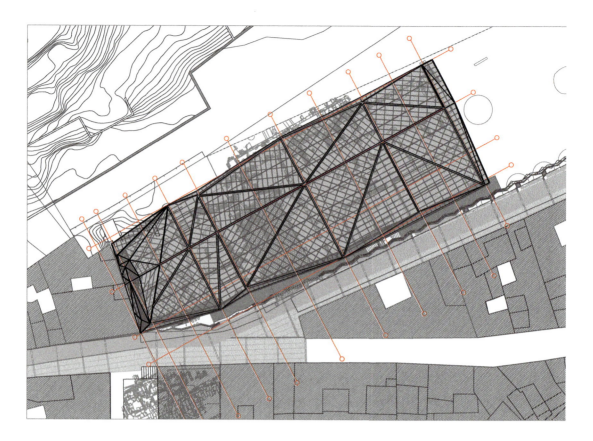

3.11
Roof plan,
Amann-Cánovas-Maruri,
El Molinete, Cartagena,
Spain, 2011.

unlike the surrounding site (both the natural topography of the hill and exposed ruins and the built fabric of the city, which rests on the ruins themselves), but also entirely responding to those two opposing habitats. The deliberate reading of the canopy structure against the ruins produces a kind of cross grain that literally stitches these two habitats together.

Roman Cartagena has its own underlying grain and edges that persist within the contemporary city, either through excavation or through continued use over time. This evolution occurs at a smaller scale and timeframe on the site of the project, but it is what makes this project so responsive to its site, both the physical conditions and cultural context. The definition of the site has evolved from the initial fence and what that was meant to achieve, to the canopy and museum, which has been profoundly shaped by the first intervention as a small part of the larger history of the city's development. The canopy, like the original fence, also continues to inhabit the edges of the site, which now encompasses the larger three-dimensional territory of the excavation area. The canopy and fence together define the site: they create legible edges to understand the history within the enclosure in a separate time and as its own entity, and they are permeable, allowing history and present, indoor and outdoor, and landscape and city to commingle.

Notes

1   For more detailed information on the history of the region, see "History of Cartagena," *Murcia Today*, http://murciatoday.com/history-of-cartagena-part-1-prehistory-to-the-argaric-culture_5849-a.html.

2   Lydia Parafianowicz, "Roman Ruins Roof," *Frame* online, March 1, 2012, www.frameweb.com/news/roman-ruins-roof.

3   Oliver Wainwright, "Canopy for Roman Site, Cartagena, Spain by Amann Cánovas Maruri Architects," Building Design UK, www.bdonline.co.uk/canopy-for-roman-site-cartagena-spain-by-amann-c%C3%A1novas-maruri-architects/5033819.article.

4   Wainwright, "Canopy for Roman Site."

5   Atxu Amann, Andrés Cánovas, and Nicolás Maruri (architects for the project), project description, October 30, 2013.

3.12
View from under the canopy, Amann-Cánovas-Maruri, El Molinete, Cartagena, Spain, 2011.

Part II

Experiencing Site

Experience involves the processing of one's senses: haptic, visual, aural, smelled, thought, or felt. How you experience a site is an intricate visceral response to the context, and it depends on your impressions, either fleeting or built up over time. While experience is individual, it is critical to scrutinize and express because it will inevitably influence the approach to a project. The way in which experience can act on the mind, unconsciously or consciously, will alter the decisions made relative to the site. Experience is also often something held in common, something that can be shared by many people. Capturing this, and understanding what is shared or personal, is difficult to analyze in a scientific sense. It can be represented so that individual impressions are communicated, or analyzed in order to determine an individual response.

4

Composite Montage

Architecture gathers meaning. It connects the things we process through our senses to our emotions and memories of other things (other moments, other places, etc.). The struggle (and what defines architecture) is in how you design something that will allow for these connections. You must be able to not only articulate the experience of senses, emotions, and memories tied to a site, but also understand how the architecture will open up the possibility of recognizing these. Kenneth Frampton, architect and historian, echoes this dilemma and offers a potential resolution:

> The specific culture of the region—that is to say, its history in both a geological and agricultural sense—becomes inscribed into the form and realization of the work. This inscription, which arises out of "in-laying" the building into the site, has many levels of significance, for it has a capacity to embody, in built form, the prehistory of the place, its archeological past and its subsequent cultivation and transformation across time. Through this layering into the site the idiosyncrasies of place find their expression without falling into sentimentality.[1]

For Frampton, architecture is capable of embodying a place: it is the host for and expression of its history and embodies our interaction with that place—what we may do on it or to shape it. Experiencing a site is the action of perceiving the physical and perceptual cues offered by this embedded history. Architect Steven Holl describes a similar concept: "Building transcends physical and functional requirements by fusing with a place, by gathering the meaning of a situation... Illumination of a site is not a simplistic replication of its 'context'; to reveal an aspect of a place may not confirm its 'appearance.'"[2] Holl's "fusing" is forged through what he calls a "metaphysical" or "poetic" link—Frampton describes this as "in-laying."

Frampton's description of the layering of a site is useful because it offers a means for beginning to unpack experiencing a site. If a site is made of layers, there exists the possibility of separating or recombining these layers to uncover, or in Holl's words, reveal an aspect of a place. These layers may not be visual and do not all exist in the same time or scale—layers are an abstraction. Also because you cannot necessarily see these layers on a site, you must understand these layers as part of the process of in-laying—you are creating abstract layers of a site to generate a design that will affect the understanding of that site in the future. However, the revelation provided by the abstraction of these layers is essential to both discovering and articulating the often intangible aspects of experience that will fundamentally shape the architecture.

Landscape architect and urban designer James Corner's work in *Taking Measures Across the American Landscape*, with aerial photographer Alex MacLean, provides an intriguingly literal translation of this idea of revealing layers within the American landscape. MacLean's photographs serve as the counterpoint of realism,[3] collapsing the "in-laying" of the site within the snapshot, so that Corner's map-drawings begin to peel apart and separate the constituent layers buried in each site studied. These map-drawings, which he later refers to as composite montages,[4] are constructed of a composite of borrowed imagery, from photographs to historic and contemporary maps/charts to other visual miscellany. The images flirt with both analysis and artwork: they are compositional in their form and clearly analytical in their content. Corner borrows the analysis buried in the notations of the maps and charts he uses, and through the composite image brings his own analysis of these drawings and the place to bear at the intersections and overlaps of the images borrowed. He is also seeking to peel apart the layers that are embedded in MacLean's photography, decrypting the "in-laying" of the site.

Windmill Topography (Figure 4.1), when stripping apart its constituent layers, is made of an inverted topographic map, several wind charts, at least three photographs at radically different scales, and two different site sections. The focal point of the image wobbles between the ovoid figure of the topography (reminiscent of the trajectory of the blades) and the carefully incised and enlarged photograph of the wind turbines on the right. This tension in the focal point brings the purpose of the work forward, highlighting the nature of the turbine as a responsive mechanism deployed in relationship to the topography that then creates its own topography in array. Red lines crisscross the topographic map and transverse site section embedding a second layer that illustrates the wind pressure vector analysis. In the lower right corner, another wind chart spurs from the foot of the image of the turbine, carving through a color photograph of the landscape as it rises to the ridge. In the upper left corner, a kind of counterbalance appears illustrating a lateral section with the turbines in elevation brought forward by a watercolor of the sky, sliced by a hand drawing of the blades. A fingernail of topography floats in the lower left, again reminding us of the trajectories of the blades. These elements slice, carve and arc through each other: the cropping and overlaying help to reveal the unseen motion of the turbine blades as well as the monumental motion of the wind sliced by the ridge.

While Frampton and Holl's arguments may be overextended to justify the wind turbine as high architecture, the composite montage significantly reveals the embodied aspects of the site—the ground, climate, location, and cultural/societal need for clean energy—in relationship to the turbine.

Corner later describes this technique when discussing the "eidetic image" in his book *Recovering Landscape*: "Composite montage is essentially an affiliative and productive technique, aimed … toward emancipation, hetero-geneity, and open-ended relations among parts."[5] Composite montage carries a multiplicity of meaning, doing what is essentially the opposite of the reductive simplification found in Corner's embedded charts and maps. Created through the appropriation of other representations, the work's open-ended nature allows a freedom in interpretation, much like the physical experience of a site where you would be experientially creating your own interpretation based on sensory and connotative response. To borrow from Holl again, the work is poetic: it associates both personal and cultural experience. The rhythm and visual presence of words in a poem can be as significant as the content and relationships contained in the words. Like a poem, there is interplay between the denotative power of the fragments within the drawing and the connotative suggestions they make by their fragmentation.

Marco Frascari, architect and theorist, describes this as a "tell-the-tale detail." Frascari, elaborating on the Beaux-Arts tradition of the *analytique*, defines the tell-the-tale detail as the piece that conceptually encompasses the whole, as the "generator" of design: "In this graphic representation of a designed or sur-veyed building the details play the predominant role. They are composed in different scales in the attempt to single out the dialogue among the parts in the making of the text of the building. Sometimes the building as a whole is present in the drawing, and generally it is represented on a minuscule scale, and so it seems a detail among details."[6] The detail is scale-relative; it is the architect that chooses through the arrangement of scale and connection on the page the signif-icance of the fragment to the whole.

James Corner's *Hoover Dam and the Colorado River* (Figure 4.2) also seeks to reveal the design "generator" through composite montage. The swooping arc of the plan of the dam divides the light and dark of the page, generating a visual tension reminiscent of the immense weight pressing against that line. An artificial crack has been opened in this plan, separating two scales of photography and a line emerges out of this fissure becoming a detail of the section of the dam wall. A figure carved out of the right side of the drawing uncovers the Colorado River extending all the way to the Davis Dam. The perpendicular lines of the dam are echoed in the void puncturing the plan, also helping to show the system to re-regulate flow along the river. The arc that is both plan and section is also the Colorado River, bringing us to the tell-the-tale detail in the Composite Montage.

VLA: Powers of Ten I (Figure 4.3) takes a different compositional approach. The Very Large Array (VLA) is a massive radio telescope on the Plains of Saint Agustin in New Mexico, made up of 27 radio antennae that can be moved into several different configurations depending on the nature of what is being observed. Because radio waves cannot be seen with the eye and are incredibly large, the telescope uses telemetry to collect the information from each antenna and calibrates it similarly to the way our mind calibrates between the information

4.2
Hoover Dam and the Colorado River,
James Corner, 1996.

received by both eyes to give us a single image. The material studied at the VLA cannot be seen, and it collects information from incredibly far sources. The composite montage is textural: the first overarching layer creates a kind of super-graphic ruler referencing the scales of measurement seen in Charles and Ray Eames's short film *Powers of Ten*,[7] which is then embedded with visual references from prehistoric art used to determine measurements of the sky, the motion of the antennae, radio images produced by the VLA, the human eye, historic maps of the globe, and so on. Cutting against and through this ruler is the plan of the VLA, slightly off axis, and a square marked as a square mile against this plan. The tracks of the VLA project beyond the ruler draw attention to the mobility of the array and its changeable configurations, as well as the extreme physical scale of the telescope on the landscape. As with the *Hoover Dam and*

Composite Montage

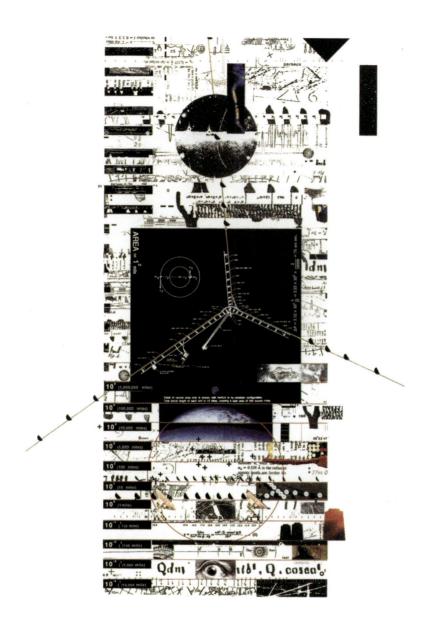

the Colorado River, the simultaneous scales at work in the drawing speak to the detail of the antennae equal to the curve of the Earth and the vast and ancient distances of emitting objects in the sky. This simultaneity effectively frames the experience of the site.

Composite imagery is not a new phenomenon—collage, montage, bricolage, decoupage, mosaic, and assemblage—all of these words describe a kind of fragmentation and reassembly into a new work. It can be seen as a primal creative act; in art, composite images have been around since the caves of Lascaux where the fragmented and repeated paintings of horses describe, recount, inventory and express the essence of the animal. This link to the very beginning of art is significant because experiencing a site, capturing it and expressing it, is fundamentally a human act. The development of composite imagery through the direct appropriation of objects follows the history of both architecture and art and comes into its own through the Surrealists and Cubists, especially in the work of Pablo Picasso and Georges Braque.[8]

In architecture, composite images that borrow from photography or other sources outside drawing emerged most prominently in the Bauhaus School. The overarching premise for these composite techniques is to borrow meaning. The act of cropping and pasting from an outside source into a new work brings the associations of the source directly into that work. Arranging these fragments into a composition forces a new consideration of the relationship between the content contained in each fragment. This can be seen in Marianne Brandt's collage *Es ist Geschmacksache* ("It is a matter of taste"), which compels you to consider the juxtaposition of the men and women's actions displayed in the collage (Figure 4.4).

Composite montage can also be an open-ended and affiliative tool to study the experience of a site as part of the design process. Antoine Predock uses both collage and modeling in his design process, to disassemble or fragment the site

4.4
Es ist Geschmacksache,
Marianne Brandt, 1926.

Galerie Berinson, Berlin.

4.5
Collage, Antoine Predock
Architect, Arizona
Science Center, Phoenix,
Arizona, USA, 1990.

in order to reassemble it and understand these fragments in a new way.[9] For Predock, like both Holl and Frampton, the site is made up of physical and metaphysical layers: "In a highway roadcut ... a sectional diagram of the earth is revealed through man's intervention ... The roadcut is a diagram of the investigative process for the making of architecture."[10] The conceptualization of slicing into the landscape as the process of making architecture is a powerful metaphor

for his collage techniques, which are an amalgam of borrowed historical and contemporary imagery stitched together with large-scale gestural sketches. His collages are both analytical and conceptual (and typically quite large), and seek to capture a kind of tell-the-tale detail to drive the project. The Arizona Science Center (Figure 4.5) "blends, in an abstract manner, influences drawn from geological events with site-specific concerns and urban opportunities. Silhouette and horizon merge with the phenomena of light, water, reflection and mirage."[11] While his words describe the building, they are an equally effective description of his collage. Images of geological formations are interlaced with images of the skyline of Phoenix, rainstorms, sunsets, an eclipse, lightning, and Arizona wildlife. Bold hatches of color taken from these images draw your eye to the blue of the water and the colors of the rock. The collage is also a large-scale sketch of the massing of the building on the site made out of these fragments—it is an architectural re-creation of the desert and its relationship to water, which is central to the museum's program and the larger site.

Predock's collage for the Hotel Santa Fe deploys a similar methodology for the project (Figure 4.6). The hotel is located in Paris, but the collage is an attempt to capture the site of the American Southwest, bringing the layers of geology, nature, and human history—both real and in myth, built and imagined—to its location at Disneyland Paris. While the building cannot claim to embody the physical site it is in in Paris, as part of an American amusement park that has been transplanted into its location in France, the collage offers a curiously unusual way of understanding a site. Predock has been characterized as a Southwestern architect—the collage is an amalgamation of his own analysis and experience of the region that is then transported and applied to an entirely different location. The "site" for this project is the Southwest, grafted into Paris like a genetically modified organism.

4.6
Collage, Antoine Predock Architect, Hotel Santa Fe, Paris, France, 1992.

The subjective quality of experiencing a site highlights some ambiguities at the core of a representation like composite montage. For example, any of the work shown in this chapter is equally culpable of using information the viewer may not understand or employ obscure visual references. The larger purpose of a technique like composite montage is to attempt to communicate the complexities of experiencing a site with an eye towards a larger design idea, and all of the works shown deliver a level of redundancy to aid in strengthening that idea. Experience occurs directly through the senses, but also requires the brain to process this raw information. Associations and connections are forged intuitively and immediately at the subconscious level; by introducing a similar visual interplay through the composite montage, a link can be made to your own experience by unpacking or delaminating the layers buried in the site. The process attempts to understand what has become seamless, embodied, in the landscape. Analogous to experiencing a site, you cannot view this type of representation once and discard it: the interpretation becomes richer with repeated viewing. The representation is composite, seeing what is there and constructing a way of seeing it, providing the generative detail that can become the design.

Notes

1   Kenneth Frampton, "Towards a Critical Regionalism: Six Points for an Architecture of Resistance," in *The Anti-Aesthetic: Essays on Postmodern Culture*, ed. Hal Foster (Port Townsend, WA: Bay Press, 1983), 26.

2   Steven Holl, *Anchoring* (New York: Princeton Architectural Press, 1989), 9.

3   For further discussion on the realism of the aerial photograph, refer to Denis Cosgrove, "The Measures of America," in *Taking Measures Across the American Landscape*, by James Corner and Alex MacLean (New Haven, CT: Yale University Press, 1996), 3–13.

4   James Corner, "Eidetic Operations and New Landscapes," in *Recovering Landscape: Essays in Contemporary Landscape Architecture*, ed. James Corner (New York: Princeton Architectural Press, 1999), 166.

5   Corner, "Eidetic Operations," 166.

6   Marco Frascari, "The Tell-the-Tale Detail," in *Theorizing a New Agenda for Architecture: An Anthology of Architectural Theory 1965–1995*, ed. Kate Nesbitt (New York: Princeton Architectural Press, 1996), 502.

7   *Powers of Ten*, documentary short film, directed and written by Charles and Ray Eames (1968; DVD: Chatsworth, CA: Image Entertainment, 2000).

8   For more information on the history of collage and composite techniques, see Brandon Taylor, *Collage: The Making of Modern Art* (New York: Thames & Hudson, 2004).

9   For more on Antoine Predock's process, see Christopher C. Mead, "Sighting the Landscape," in *Antoine Predock*, by Antoine Predock (Seoul: C3 Design Group, 2001), 8–23.

10 Antoine Predock, in *Roadcut: The Architecture of Antoine Predock*, by Christopher C. Mead (Albuquerque, NM: University of New Mexico Press, 2011), 5.

11 Predock, *Antoine Predock*, 64.

5

Topography

The ground's significance to architecture cannot be understated. Architect Vittorio Gregotti captures the essence of this when discussing the ground in relationship to the foundations of architecture: "that first and secret surface of contact with the earth on which the work rests, that first connection that distributes the force of the load, dispersing it into the ground, is obviously itself both the result and the beginning of all construction projects."[1] While buildings may artificially suspend us from it, architecture is fundamentally created in relationship to the ground[2]— it is also the datum by which we experience architecture. It is something that is physically *there*, with or without us, and at the same time more than its physical composition. Robin Dripps, writing on the complexities of the ground, proposes this idea:

> Metaphorically, ground refers to the various patterns of physical, intellectual, poetic, and political structure that intersect, overlap, and weave together to become the context for human thought and action … It is easy to understand how the earth's rough and bumpy surfaces, its uncertain and shifting fixity and its damp porosity could be considered qualities that would destabilize physical, political, and even psychological equilibrium.[3]

His description implies that the trace of human history (astronomic, geologic, cultural, etc.)—cultural context—is embodied in the ground. We understand this easily through the field of archeology, which literally digs into the earth to reveal our history, but it is often neglected when considering architecture since it is simpler to see a building/object as the cultural artifact in juxtaposition to the ground. But the idea that the ground is as *made* as the things on it equates what we call the natural and the built; it also allows us to perceive all context as a part of the ground. Discussing the significance of nature to architecture, the architect Tadao Ando conflates the natural and the built as a potential design strategy: "Contemporary architecture ... has a role to play in providing people with architectural places that make them feel the presence of nature. When it does this, architecture transforms nature through abstraction, changing its meaning."[4] The ground is a physical entity that carries with it the trace of its cultural interaction, so that understanding what it *is* (as an abstraction of what is there) is essential to how it is translated into a representation.

Topography—the mapping or charting of the ground—has a long-standing notational history embedded in the technical art of map-making, cutting radially from the earth's core through the landscape to reveal the profile of change. This representational method is made infinitely more complex because land does not operate according to simple geometric rules; it stretches beyond the scope of any site, and its undulations and surface changes can be difficult to read with your eye. In architecture, topography, as a plan made of profile lines to imply complex surface geometry, is a compelling tool to understand any complicated solid, but in school and in the field we are typically not taught how to physically survey the landscape to create these profiles relative to the earth's core. We are taught how to read, interpret and manipulate the topographic lines taken from a survey to our own ends and understanding. As architect Raimund Abraham suggests:

> It is the conquest of the site, the transformation of its topographical nature, that manifest the ontological roots of architecture. The process of design is only a secondary and subsequent act, whose purpose is to reconcile and harmonize the consequences of the initial intervention, collision, and negation.[5]

Architect Álvaro Siza Vieira's large body of work can be seen as an evolving investigation into understanding, acknowledging and revealing the ground of a site to shape your experience of the architecture. Portugal, and in particular northern Portugal, is almost entirely made up of mountains and coastline: the shifting topography of the mountains is a perpetual counterpoint to the flatness of the coast. Much of Siza's work was designed for this part of the country, and by default it must confront the topography. What is intriguing about Siza's approach is that there is an almost technical consistency about how he records and represents topography. In one of his first well-known projects after the Boa Nova Tea House, Siza designed and built a municipal swimming pool and changing facility on the beach at Leça da Palmeira, the Piscina da Praia de Leça, that sits along the coastal road that leads into Porto and the mouth of the Douro River. Siza describes his process as an effort to "...exploit as far as possible the

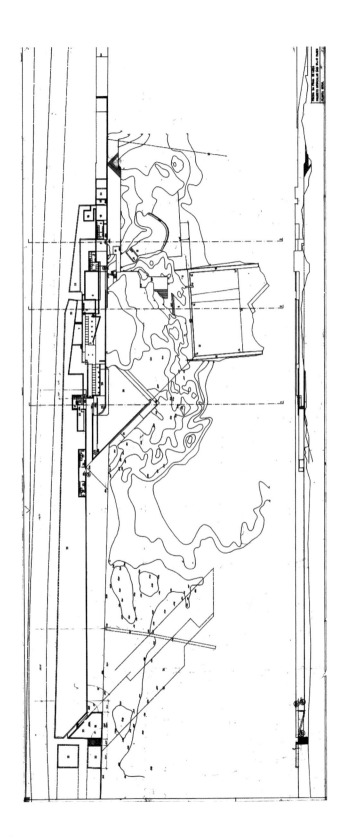

5.1
Site plan and elevation,
Álvaro Siza Vieira,
Piscina da Praia de Leça,
Leça da Palmeira,
Portugal, 1966.

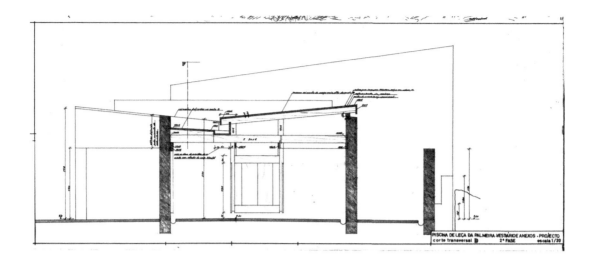

5.2
Transverse section,
Álvaro Siza Vieira,
Piscina da Praia de Leça,
Leça da Palmeira,
Portugal, 1966.

5.3
[Opposite] Initial
sketches, Álvaro Siza
Vieira, Chiado
Redevelopment, Lisbon,
Portugal, 1990.

natural conditions which had, so to speak, already started to design the swim-ming pool…with such walls as were strictly necessary. In this way we managed to integrate the landscape and the building…."[6]

Siza worked meticulously to record the locations of the rocks and his notated spot elevations throughout the landscape can be seen in the site/main floor plan (Figure 5.1). The project resembles a wall in plan, mitigating the flat constructed topography of the road and the free-form profiles of the rocky beach; in built form, you walk along an exterior path within that wall, inhabiting the liminal space between two topographic conditions of natural and built before emerging onto the beach. Often choosing to use clean line drawings, Siza is particular in setting his drawings in relationship to each other—the topographic lines in his site plan translate to an elevation of the shore, where the subtleties of the topography on the beach become compressed into the line of the shore in elevation. Kenneth Frampton, architect and historian, remarked on this project that "we are confronted with a topographic conception which organizes the entire project. Here everything turns on a subtle mediation between the coastal road, a rock-strewn site and the open sea … Thus everything is a part of the earthwork in one way or another."[7] Because the project is located at the literal edge of Portugal, in the space between the coastal road and the shoreline, the project becomes the experience of inhabiting that edge through the controlled descent from the road to the sea. The transverse section (Figure 5.2) reveals this descent downwards, always from the road to the coast, literally claiming the topography as the building. While the change in topography is less than three meters, the haptic immersion of this descent is experientially necessary.

In his work, Álvaro Siza repeats the technique of rigorous topographic notation that translates into a comprehensive unfolding of the site into two-dimensional drawings, regardless of the natural or built context. His master plan of the redevelopment of the Chiado area in Lisbon, Portugal, reflects this design

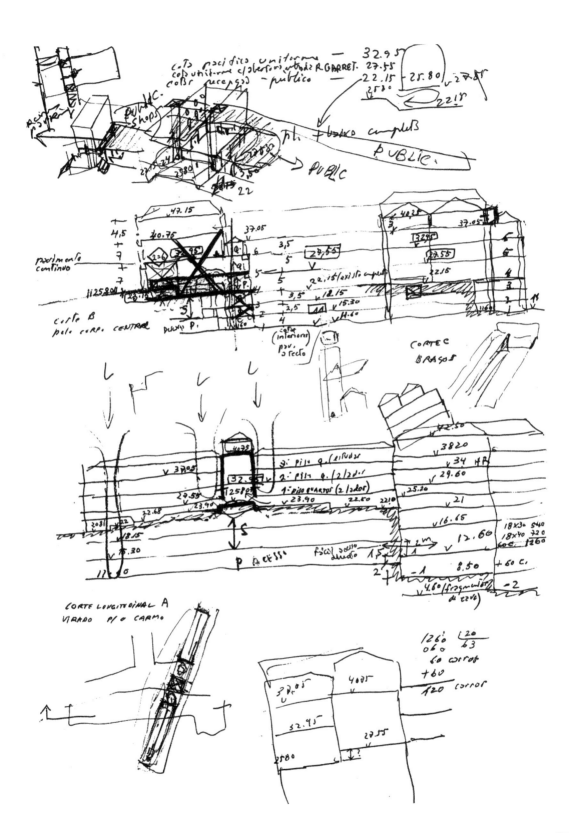

Topography

5.4
Plan and unfolded
elevations, Álvaro
Siza Vieira, Chiado
Redevelopment, Lisbon,
Portugal, 1990.

Experiencing Site

process much later in his career in a radically different context. Lisbon exists at the mouth of the Tagus River and its topography is dominated by several hills that spill down into a larger basin (the Baixa) towards the sea: the Chiado neighborhood straddles the edge of one these hills. It is incredibly dense—densely populated and densely built up—and the streets can be quite narrow and steep; this was part of the reason the fire of 1988 was able to spread so quickly and damage so much of the neighborhood. Siza's redevelopment is indicative of his own trepidation to rebuild without replicating or eradicating the demolished context. Similar to the pools at Leça, the project evolves around your path along a steeply sloped alley, which is described by Siza as: "A stark hole, without frontage or molding, an unexpected hole, a sort of incomplete funnel that embraces a splendid flight of steps, before the great deterioration that has produced incomparable rotundities and strange patches of plaster."[8]

The redevelopment is a restoration of the street front, but it is also a path that rejoins the history of the neighborhood to its buildings, new and old. This path can be seen in his early sketches on the project (Figure 5.3), where he again systematically notates spot elevations to understand how this path weaves through the block. The path can be seen ascending through and in relationship to the various floors, each at a specific elevation. This translates into the sections and elevations that unfold from the overall plan, illustrating the dramatic shifting topography belied in plan (Figure 5.4). The jogged section below the plan reveals the path as it meanders away from the public street and through the neighboring buildings to the ruins of the Carmo Church. Notated in his sketches, there is a visible tension between public and private space as this path breaches the city block, and the sections show a clear intent regarding the path's changing height to the interior floors.

Siza's work responds to its site by the literal integration of the landscape, both urban and natural. His work is structured around your experience, always conscious of your movement through the project/site. Juxtaposed to this approach is the work of Dominique Perrault. Like Siza, Perrault's work returns consistently to a larger topographic idea, reinforced by his representational strategies. The Bibliothèque Nationale in Paris, one of his seminal early works, sits on the southern bank of the Seine in the thirteenth arrondissement, directly facing the water. As seen in his initial conceptual sketches for the project (Figure 5.5), Perrault chose to push the building into the ground to create a sunken courtyard at the base of the library, minimizing the overall mass of the towers as well as producing a large open space at the level of the river.

The project is as much about the public space that could be created with a constructed landmass as it is about working to frame the void made by the towers that emerge from that mass. The plan (Figure 5.6) reveals the building at the lower level, where the topographic lines of the constructed hills in this submerged courtyard play against the rigidity of the shelving in the library, framing a more intimate space despite the scale of the project. The section (Figure 5.7)

5.5
Conceptual sketch,
Dominique Perrault,
Bibliothèque Nationale
de France, Paris, France,
1995.

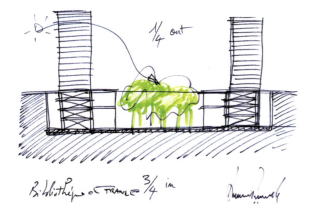

5.6
Plan, Dominique Perrault
Architecture, Biblio-
thèque Nationale de
France, Paris, France,
1995.

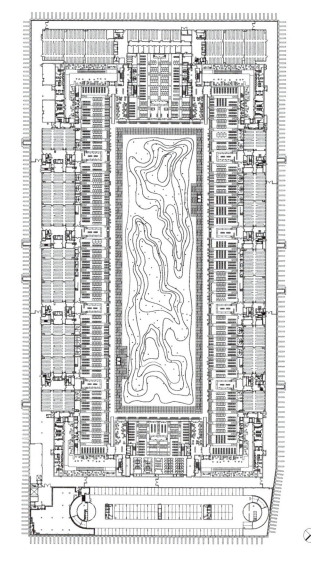

Plan du Raz-de-jardin et des Salles de lecture de recherche
Garden level and Research reading rooms plan

5.7
Section, Dominique
Perrault Architecture,
Bibliothèque Nationale
de France, Paris, France,
1995.

Coupe est - ouest
Section east - west

0 5 10   20   50

5.9
[Opposite] Master plan,
Dominique Perrault
Architecture, Velodrome
and Olympic Swimming
Pool, Berlin, Germany,
1999.

depicts the open space at the river level, which serves as a broader circulation area to the Seine and for the city at large. Perrault deliberately produces a topographic change in the relatively flat site by manipulating the ground, literally constructing ground out of the building, which is a constant in Perrault's work, and, like Siza, can be seen as a kind of continuous evolution through his projects.

Four years after the completion of the Bibliothèque, Perrault designed and built the Olympic Velodrome and Olympic Swimming Pool in Berlin for the 2000 Summer Olympic Games that helped to mark the reunification of East and West Germany. The initial conceptual sketches of this project (Figure 5.8), similar to the Bibliothèque, push the mass of the building into the earth, again taking advantage of the relatively subtle slope of the terrain of the existing site. Because of the two opposing forms dictated by the program and the complexities of knitting into the existing city, Perrault chose to literally bury both the velodrome and pool underneath an artificially built-up and flattened landscape covering two blocks, which is planted with an apple orchard throughout the constructed site. The master plan (Figure 5.9) shows the scale of the project in the city: the western edge of the site smoothly transitions to the roof at the grade of the street, subtly allowing the terrain to slope down a full story to the level of the trains on the eastern edge where the roof is legible as a constructed surface. The section (Figure 5.10) unveils the velodrome and pool hidden under the constructed landmass of the orchard, still reading as if they have been implanted into craters made in the roof/orchard.

Perrault's thinking is almost polemical regarding the relationship of site and architecture: "No idea of opposition between landscape—perception and construction of the land—and object—fragment of the land—has any place in the teaching of Architecture."[9] He sees his work as an outgrowth or extension of the

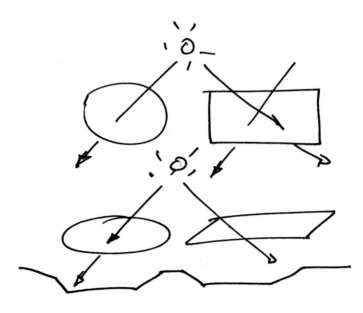

5.8
Conceptual sketch,
Dominique Perrault,
Olympic Velodrome and
Olympic Swimming Pool,
Berlin, Germany, 1999.

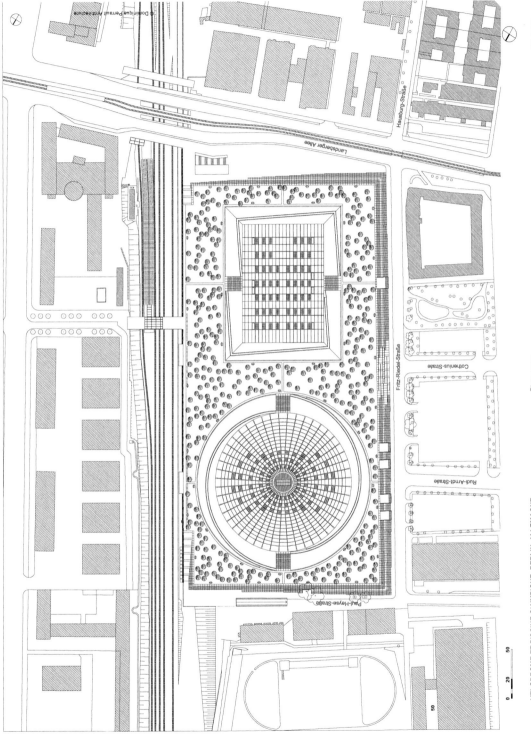

DPA

Landsberger Allee

Hausburg-Straße

Fritz-Riedel-Straße

Cotheniusstraße

Rudi-Arndt-Straße

Paul-Heyse-Straße

VELODROME ET PISCINE OLYMPIQUE, BERLIN, ALLEMAGNE
Dominique Perrault Architecture

Plan masse
Masterplan

0   20   50

50

5.10
Section, Dominique
Perrault Architecture,
Velodrome and Olympic
Swimming Pool, Berlin,
Germany, 1999.

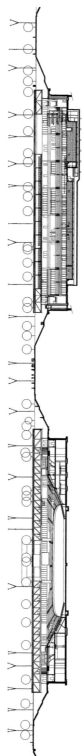

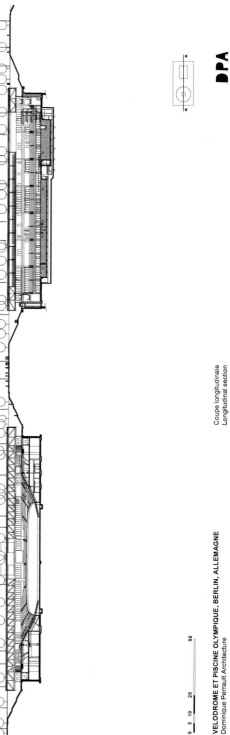

Coupe longitudinale
Longitudinal section

VELODROME ET PISCINE OLYMPIQUE, BERLIN, ALLEMAGNE
Dominique Perrault Architecture

0 5 10   20   50

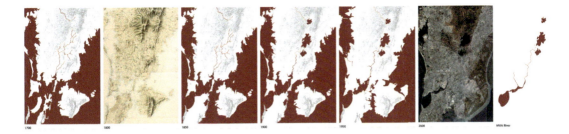

land, but it is also about perceiving the constructed landscape created. His conception of topography, distinct from Álvaro Siza, is captured within his initial sketches, almost as if he intended you to see the sketch containing the project. For Perrault, "The design process, understood as interaction between idea and place, determines ... the conscious transformation of a preexisting order in the place."[10] Siza and Perrault both perceive the land as the embodiment of its context, but this is manifest in Perrault's work in radically different ways. Where Siza's work can be seen as negotiating terrain—moving you through the landscape—Perrault's work becomes the perceived construction of the land, and at the same time the negation of that constructed land through designed voids.

The work of Anuradha Mathur and Dilip da Cunha offers a distinct counterpoint on the conception of topography and its representation. Their projects emerge directly from mapping out and understanding the ground, as both a solid and in relationship to water. Their large research and design project/exhibition SOAK: Mumbai in an Estuary (Figure 5.11) centers on the historical interpretations of Mumbai through maps that have often mislabeled or misinterpreted the "location" of the Mithi River as it empties into the sea: "The articulation of a line between the land and sea has largely gone unnoticed, and the view from above that facilitated its drawing in maps has become the taken-for-granted visualization of Mumbai's terrain."[11] The city of Mumbai rests on the delta of the Mithi River, and is subject to shifting water levels according to the seasons. Over time, the river delta area became increasingly built up, in part because the city grew, and in part because the maps of the city laid claim to this transitional territory as solid ground. "They [British surveyors] therefore pursued their task in 'fair weather,' when edges between land and water were more visible."[12] Mathur and da Cunha's maps of Mumbai trace the river over time, to what it is visible today, inevitably leading to disastrous flooding conditions that occur during the rainy seasons. Moving from this historical tracery, they began to chart the delta not as an outline, but through a series of transverse sections that could more easily visualize what cannot be considered a line where water begins (Figure 5.12). Some topography may be easily seen—on hillsides, valleys, cliffs and edges—but the subtler topography in what may seem a flat landscape can be more powerfully affecting than a mountain range.

What is interesting about Mathur and da Cunha's work, especially in relation to both Siza and Perrault, is their design projects emerge directly from an analysis

5.11
Making the Mithi,
Anuradha Mathur and
Dilip da Cunha, SOAK:
Mumbai in an Estuary,
2009.

5.12
Sections of Mumbai,
Anuradha Mathur and
Dilip da Cunha, SOAK:
Mumbai in an Estuary,
2009.

Experiencing Site

and understanding of the conditions of the ground; it produces the methodology for design. Siza's method can be seen in the recording and unfolding of the land to understand its three-dimensional qualities in carefully selected two-dimensional planes. Perrault works principally through conceptual sketches, with less concern for the precision of the undulation in the landscape than for the larger topographic move. Mathur and da Cunha's work is serial: transverse sections dissect the landscape in reaction to the problem of the ambiguity of the collapsed planar profiles of topography. Common to all of these architects' design processes is that they work directly from the site to their proposal. Analysis, recording, and observing is not set aside and then brought to bear on the project later. These projects all intend to merge with the ground through a careful balance between understanding what is *there*, and what wants to be. These projects cannot be removed from where they are; they are site specific in a way that these projects lose meaning if repositioned.

Notes

1   Vittorio Gregotti, *Architecture: Means and Ends*, trans. Lydia G. Cochrane (Chicago, IL: University of Chicago Press, 2010), 80.

2   In this chapter, I use the terms "ground," "earth," and "topography" relatively interchangeably. For a more specific discussion about the differences between earth, globe, and world, see Denis Cosgrove, "Imperial and Poetic Globe," in his *Apollo's Eye: A Cartographic Genealogy of the Earth in the Western Imagination* (Baltimore, MD: Johns Hopkins University Press, 2001), 1-28.

3   Robin Dripps, "Groundwork," in *Site Matters: Design Concepts, Histories, and Strategies*, ed. Andrea Kahn and Carol J. Burns (New York: Routledge, 2005), 59.

4   Tadao Ando, "Toward New Horizons in Architecture," in *Theorizing a New Agenda for Architecture: An Anthology of Architectural Theory 1965–1995*, ed. Kate Nesbitt (New York: Princeton Architectural Press, 1996), 460.

5   Raimund Abraham, "Negation and Reconciliation," in Nesbitt, *Theorizing a New Agenda for Architecture*, 465.

6   Álvaro Siza, "Leça de Palmeira," in *Álvaro Siza: Complete Works*, by Kenneth Frampton (London: Phaidon Press, 2000), 82.

7   Frampton, *Álvaro Siza: Complete Works*, 15–16.

8   Álvaro Siza, "The Chiado," in Frampton, *Álvaro Siza: the Complete Works*, 356.

9   Álvaro Siza, in *Siza: Architecture Writings*, ed. Antonio Angelillo (Milan: Skira, 1997), 29–30.

10   Laurent Stalder, "Projection of the Mind and Protection of the Body," in his *Projects and Architecture: Dominique Perrault* (Milan: Electa Architecture, 2000), 18.

11   Anuradha Mathur and Dilip da Cunha, "The Sea and Monsoon Within: A Mumbai Manifesto," in *Ecological Urbanism*, ed. Mohsen Mostafavi and Gareth Doherty (Baden: Lars Mueller Publishers with Harvard University, Graduate School of Design, 2010–2011), 194.

12   Mathur and da Cunha, "The Sea and Monsoon Within," 196.

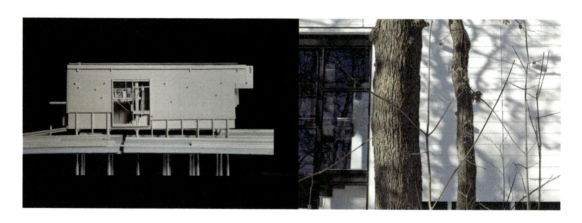

6.1
Model of the house (*left*)
and fragment of shadows
on the east façade (*right*),
Bruce A. Johnson, White
House, Lake of the
Ozarks, Missouri, USA,
2006.

6

Case Study

White House—Lake of the Ozarks, USA

The Lake of the Ozarks was created in 1931 with the installation of the Bagnell Hydroelectric Dam on the Osage River in the Ozark Mountains of Missouri. The lake, seen aerially, resembles an immense and bloated river, and extends more than 90 miles over four counties (Figure 6.2). Beyond its significance supplying electric power to the region, it, along with Truman Lake to the west (which is also a dammed portion of the Osage River), have become a prominent vacation destination in the Midwest because of what are now hundreds miles of mostly privately owned shoreline.[1]

6.2
Site diagram of the Lake of the Ozarks region showing the site relative to Truman Lake, Lake of the Ozarks, and existing waterways.

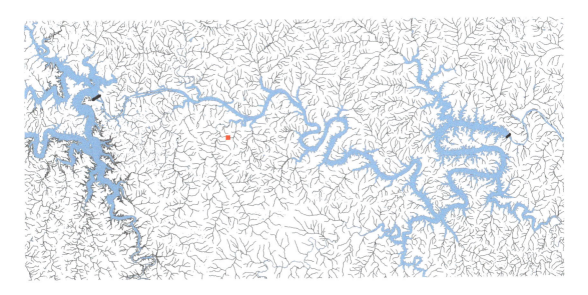

What can be difficult to understand from the air, but is evident in the fingers and meander of the lake, is that the Ozarks are filled with rolling hills and steep rocky cliffs. The geology of the area where the Lake of the Ozarks is situated contains not only the waterways associated with the dammed lake, but also a prolific number of streams that run through its valleys creating sinkholes, caves and springs. The forests in the area harbor their own history: today, these forests are predominantly made up of new growth oak trees, creating dense thickets of closely packed small-trunked trees. Prior to European settlement however, Missouri was almost entirely pine forest as well as oak savannah. After the arrival of new settlements, rail transportation lines built through the area used the forests to make wooden ties, and with the boom of the lumber industry at the turn of the century, all but a few acres of this virgin forest had been milled. After 1920, forest conservation efforts and fire prevention helped to rebuild the forests to what can be seen today.[2] The area is now a blend of agricultural lands, dense woods with sparse residential development, and carved out beach communities around the lake (Figure 6.3).

Designer–builder Bruce Johnson responded to this context in a strategic way when designing and building a modest home that looks over a small dammed stream in the area. This house is a unique perspective relative to experiencing the site because Johnson not only designed the house for its setting, he built the entire house on the site. His experience not only impacted the overall design scheme, it continued to hold sway through the process of construction. The foundations and overall site plan offer a glimpse into his response to the conditions of the site. The typical method most homebuilders in the area would choose to begin a home is by carving out an ample clearing that lays bare the house from the woods. Johnson, however, was careful to preserve as many of the trees as possible that surround the house. The lower canopy was thinned to remove fire risks, but the trees, especially on the south side, were maintained as much as possible.

From the site plan (Figure 6.4), the house sits off the main road, and a clearing can be seen which is largely masked by trees: the septic system and leach field were strategically placed on the north side, creating an intimate clearing that offers views to the small meadow from the back end of the house where the bedrooms are located. Because of the rocky characteristics of the ground, he chose to place the house on piers instead of attempting to chisel out a more normative foundation type. Eighteen power poles, used as footings, were dug into the ground so that the house skims the surface of the forest floor. In essence, the house rests on eighteen reclaimed trees that have been reburied in the earth, making the house an outgrowth of the surrounding forest.

The topography of the landscape also contributes to the experience of the site. The house is situated on a kind of ledge that has been carved away by the stream and runoff water that now contribute to the pond located in the valley below. The area directly surrounding the house is quite level, belying the drama

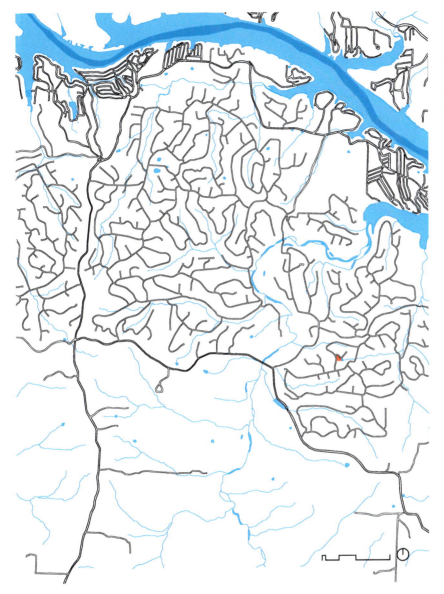

6.3
Site diagram of the area showing the abrupt transitions from agricultural lands to semi-developed forest to intensive private lakeshore developments.

that unfolds beyond it. Your procession to the house helps to stage your experience of the topography: the entryway is eroded from the north and west-facing roof/wall, hinting at the interior and the forest beyond (Figure 6.5). You walk up into the house on a shallow ramp and are confronted with trees; the ground has slipped away so that you feel you are floating in the forest. Walking around the exterior, this idea is further reinforced: the flat white plane of the east façade appears to float off the ground, as if it is pulling away from the earth.

Case Study: White House—Lake of the Ozarks, USA

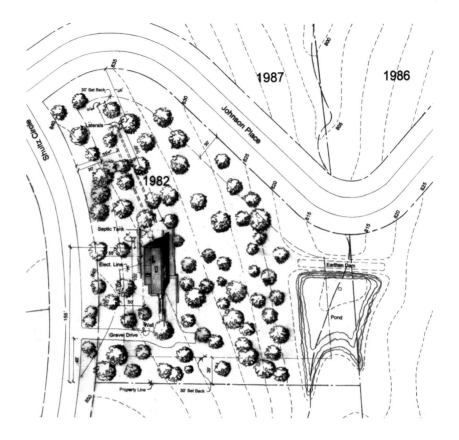

The form of the house considers the structural vernacular of barns and other rural structures. Using an asymmetrical gambrel (broken double gable) allows the roof to cascade down the west side/road-facing elevation. The structure is essentially a tube-like construction that ties the floor to the walls and roof, while a reading of the exterior shows that there are two distinct sides to the form. From the road, the house's dark shingles easily camouflage it from passersby, and make it difficult to discern as a volume. A central aperture and several smaller openings break the monumentality of the east façade's large white wall (Figure 6.6). The house is two stories on both the north and south ends, and the middle of the house is a vaulted space centered on the large east façade aperture, broken by a bridge that connects both ends. Every space is engaged with its own relationship with the outside, whether facing south to overlook the driveway and walkway into the house, north to face the clearing created by the leach field, or east looking through the trees to the pond below (Figure 6.7).

The backdrop of dense oak trees was a prime fascination of Johnson's, where he worked to unveil the experience of continuous transformation over the course of the day with the changing wind and light, and over the course of the year through the seasonal shifts in the foliage. The exterior east façade with

6.5
Exterior view of the
eroded entryway, Bruce
A. Johnson, White
House, Lake of the
Ozarks, Missouri, USA,
2006.

its monolithic proportions and white paint become the canvas for the forest, a kind of billboard of changeable shadows (Figure 6.8). The large aperture that breaks the east façade carries the shadows into the interior, where the play of the white structure and walls in the house distributes, alters and diverts the shadows of the trees. Over the seasons, the hues change, adapting to the color of the foliage (Figure 6.9). The project is also about your experience with it,

Case Study: White House—Lake of the Ozarks, USA

much like land artist Walter de Maria's work *The Lightning Field*: you are required to overnight at the installation in order to properly experience the work of art. The intimate inside spaces of this White House have a constant and changing interplay with the surrounding forest, and your perception of the house changes with its cycles.

Because Johnson physically built the project on site, the fragmentation and transformation first introduced by the reflections of the trees is carried further into the construction through his use of reclaimed materials. From the foundations as power poles, Johnson continued the reinvention of wood products throughout the house using a construction technique more typical in older homes to reinforce framing. This technique typically sisters new wood framing to existing framing in a house to shore up spans and openings (see Figure 6.10). Johnson inverted this process by using recycled framing in the house as much as possible, sistering mismatched lengths of wood together to achieve the heights and spacing required. New wood framing was reserved for the principal loading members. While the house sits lightly on the land, its relationship with the exterior builds an internal formal vocabulary that is very much like the structure of a fugue, intertwining and building on the counterpoint of the exterior context. The construction technique the designer employed allowed him to carefully consider the placement of structural and partition components in the two-story space, especially in the larger vaulted area. The

6.6
Exterior view of the east façade, Bruce A. Johnson, White House, Lake of the Ozarks, Missouri, USA, 2006.

Experiencing Site

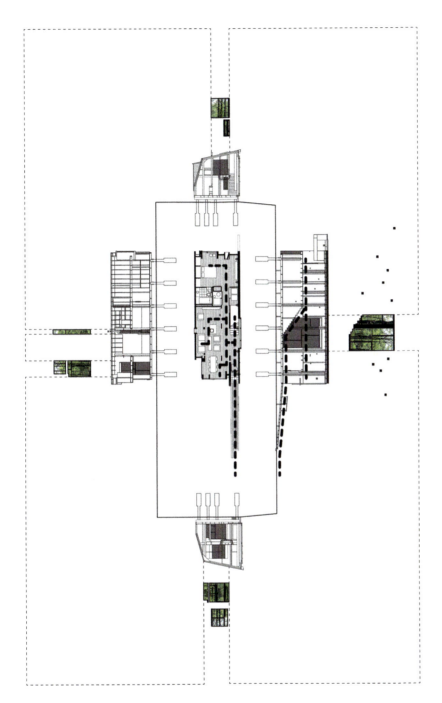

6.7
Composite drawing of
the plan and unfolded
elevations and apertures,
Bruce A. Johnson, White
House, Lake of the
Ozarks, Missouri, USA,
2006.

6.8
Composite drawing—
translation from exterior
reflection and shadow to
east elevation and
interior, Bruce A.
Johnson, White House,
Lake of the Ozarks,
Missouri, USA, 2006.

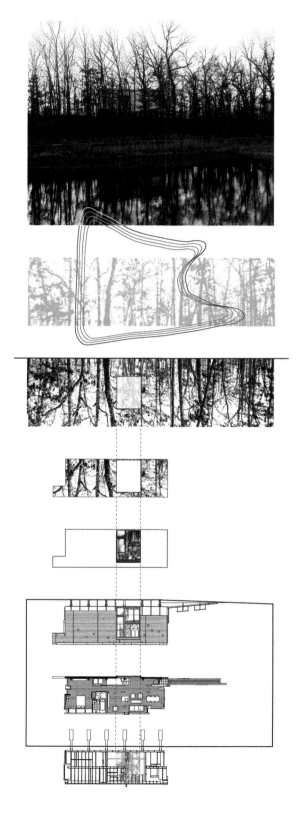

6.9
Interior view showing the
change in seasons, Bruce
A. Johnson, White
House, Lake of the
Ozarks, Missouri, USA,
2006.

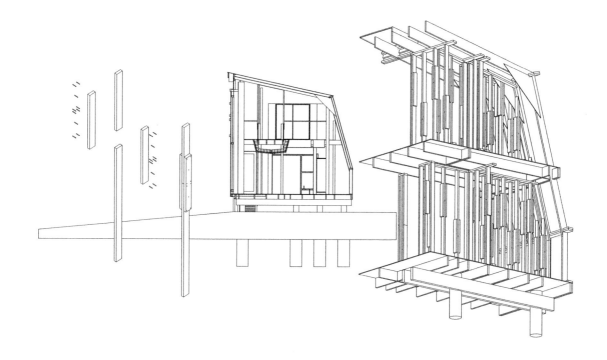

6.10
Axonometric of the
house construction,
Bruce A. Johnson, White
House, Lake of the
Ozarks, Missouri, USA,
2006.

intricacy and idiosyncrasy of the placement of columns, pilasters and partitions help to recreate the experience of walking through the woods, forcing you to navigate around vertical elements to arrive at spaces that feel like clearings in the forest.

Bruce Johnson worked to construct the house while simultaneously considering the idea of its construction, as seen in his composite drawings (Figure 6.11). The context is literally brought into the drawing through photography. Reminiscent of Gordon Matta-Clark's work, Johnson's composite drawings are a way to envision your movement through the house, perpetuating the fragmentation and synthesis of the experience. Writing on Matta-Clark's work, James Attlee states, "Matta-Clark himself was more interested, as he put it in his notebooks, in converting a building into a state of mind."[3] In a similar fashion, Bruce Johnson builds a state of mind out of the literal fragments of previous construction to produce a new experience, a new reality, welded together by what he refers to as "the power of paint."[4] This experience unfolds through the careful lacing of photography into the drawings of the building to reinforce the intentions of the overall scheme. The project cannot be understood with a single photograph, diagram, or statement. It requires a visual reading, through the act of walking as well as the careful contemplation only found at rest. It is extremely fitting for a house deep in the woods—the experience of the interior must match the power and sense of discovery outside, while also contending with the programmatic needs of a house intentionally in isolation. Each space feels far from a neutral backdrop. The site refuses to end at the front door of

6.11
Composite montage,
Bruce A. Johnson, White
House, Lake of the
Ozarks, Missouri, USA,
2006.

Case Study: White House—Lake of the Ozarks, USA

the project—you are constantly confronted with the changing context of the woods around you once you have entered it. You understand and feel the presence of the design: the house challenges you to engage the limits of your flexibility experiencing the interior, as a visitor and as an inhabitant. This experience refuses to allow you to behold the object placed in the landscape; instead, you read the project as a kind of the seamless threshold from built to natural.

Notes

1   Michael Gillespie, "Bagnell Dam Facts and Figures," 2005, www.lakehistory.info/dam facts.html.
2   James M. Guildin, "A History of Forest Management in the Ozark Mountains," in *Pioneer Forest: A Half Century of Sustainable Uneven-aged Forest Management in the Missouri Ozark*, by James M Guldin, Greg F. Iffrig, and Susan L. Flader (General Technical Report, SRS108; Asheville, NC: U.S. Department of Agriculture, Forest Service, Southern Research Station, 2008), 3–8.
3   James Attlee, "Towards Anarchitecture: Gordon Matta-Clark and Le Corbusier," *Tate Papers*, no. 7, (Spring 2007), www.tate.org.uk/research/publications/tate-papers/towards-anarchitecture-gordon-matta-clark-and-le-corbusier.
4   Bruce A. Johnson, interview with author, November 29, 2012.

Part III

Spatializing Site

In a sparsely built up or rural setting, space dominates built form. In densely built-up areas, such as cities, space takes on its own unique character in response to the buildings that create it. This space is not interior, but it is also built—it is often public, but does not have to be. There is a kind of etiquette to the movement, behavior, and rhythm to this fundamentally liminal space. It is stuck between and appropriated by all those that use it, either by easement, right of way or simple arrogation. This space is also structured, either by the design of planners and architects, or by the more tactical response of neighbors following neighbors. A site in an urban condition may be complex to analyze and understand because it must grapple with the nature of the space that it is contributing to. There is a distinct difference between the space created by an intersection of L'Eixample blocks in Barcelona and the tight grid of downtown Philadelphia, or the curving ambiguity of the City of London. Architecture creates these spaces through aggregation—it is nearly always a smaller piece of a much larger "fabric" or "texture" that will enable a larger, networked space made up of the gaps, voids, thresholds, paths and transitions. It is absolutely critical to be able to analyze what this space is—what creates it, and what characterizes it—in the urban context, because any design will contribute to that space. It can be considered simultaneously at multiple scales, as a whole or by its individual edges—analyzing it is a way of learning the site, but also designing the site.

7

Figure Ground

The figure ground, a traditional planimetric analysis of solid and void, stretches back through the history of mapping as a specific tool to illustrate the city. Giambattista Nolli's *Pianta Grande di Roma*, produced in 1748, is a pivotal example of the implementation of this technique often discussed by architects, urbanists and theorists.[1] Without going into a lengthy analysis of this particular map, what is significant about it is its precision and its systematic recording of the city of Rome. Nolli was commissioned by the Pope to take stock of the holdings of the church within the city. This led Nolli to draw out the first floor plan of every church, while indicating every other building as a black mass, and every street or open space as a void. The city is transformed in this reading, showing a dense network of streets that open seamlessly into piazzas. This technique illustrates connected buildings as whole masses relative to the connected network of white space made of up streets and open areas. It can simplify the complexities of the city to a relatively small number of relationships, so the technique of the figure ground is pervasive in mapping cities.[2]

Because the figure ground reduces whole cities to black masses separated by white voids, the critical feature exposed by this technique is space. The space of the city is created by vertical obstructions (like buildings) that you see when you walk down a street: these obstructions limit your views. Space is implied by the proximity of vertical obstructions to each other, which can be more difficult to perceive at street level, but which a planimetric analysis reveals quickly. The two basic relationships of verticality and width help shape our own reactions to that space—the sense of grandeur on a broad avenue versus the feeling of unease in a dark narrow alley with an imperceptible end, the intimacy of a small square versus the awe of a grand piazza. While many other features can influence our perception of urban space, this height to width relationship drives and shapes how we characterize a city; the technique of figure ground also makes it possible to compare one city to another.

Colin Rowe and Fred Koetter's 1979 book *Collage City* is a thesis on the problem of Modern architecture, and why there may never be a "city of Modern Architecture."[3] The dilemma for these authors is that the Modern city depends on erasing the past, through utopian or dystopian rationale: "the results of science fiction … usually suffer from the same conditions which plague the *ville radieuse*—disregard for context, distrust of the social continuum, the use of symbolic utopian models for literal purposes, [and] the assumption that the existing city will be made to go away."[4]

Their thesis led to a figure ground analysis of many cities, looking specifically at the traditional European city in juxtaposition to Modernist architecture meant to evoke the *idea* of city. These two poles "present themselves as the alternative reading of some Gestalt diagram illustrating the fluctuations of the figure-ground phenomenon … and, in both cases, the fundamental ground promotes an entirely different category of figure—in one the *object*, in the other *space*."[5]

Using the figure ground of Corbusier's Saint-Dié master plan (Figure 7.1) and the figure ground of Parma, Italy (Figure 7.2), Rowe and Koetter lay bare the dramatic difference between the amount of void space in each drawing. For the authors, Modern architecture had a "widespread tendency to space worship"[6] by considering the object in space, rather than the space made by the object. The concept of a Gestalt diagram, referring to the psychological effect where you perceive organization within individual parts, is at the core of the problem. The discrete masses in the figure ground of Saint-Dié all have individual definition, but fail to define the space between them, while the close-packed masses in the figure ground of Parma reveal a distinct white figure that is as defined as the masses in the drawing. *Collage City* is a treatise on the space of the city: Rowe and Koetter use the figure ground to demonstrate the importance of the connected space of the street, which is created by the close relationships of building masses.

The traditional city is "the solid and continuous matrix or texture giving energy to its reciprocal condition, the specific space; the ensuing square and street acting as some kind of public relief valve and providing some condition of legible structure."[7] This ideal city, for Rowe and Koetter, is created by its specific space. No one building can make a city, but buildings contribute to the texture that creates a city. This implies that any piece of architecture is only as significant as its place within that texture. While potentially self-evident to urbanites, this concept can be difficult to understand as an architect, because it entails surrendering the notion that your building can stand apart and be looked at separately and in relationship to the city. Since *Collage City* was published in the late 1970s, Rowe and Koetter's valuing of the space of the traditional city over a city of

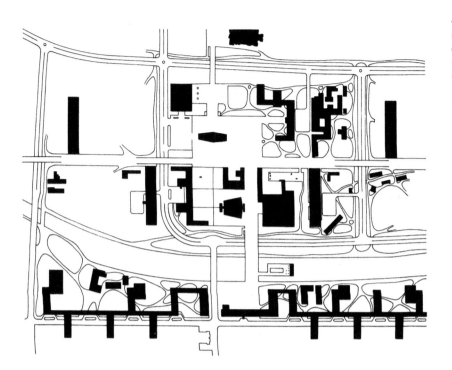

7.1
Figure ground of Le
Corbusier's Saint-Dié
master plan. Colin Rowe
and Fred Koetter, *Collage
City* (Cambridge, MA:
MIT Press, 1979), 62.

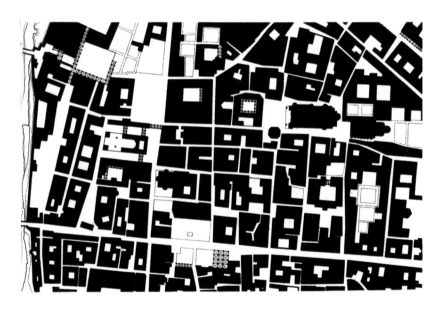

7.2
Figure ground of Parma,
Italy. Colin Rowe and
Fred Koetter, *Collage City*
(Cambridge, MA: MIT
Press, 1979), 62.

isolated objects in a continuous void could be (and has been) challenged or
revised today. With the prolific amount of isolated object city-building that has
been done in both the Middle East and Asia over the past 35 years, as well as the
maturing of the American city as a network of suburban enclaves, there is a great
deal of variation between the two poles proposed by Saint-Dié and Parma. But the

technique of the figure ground was invaluable to frame the argument of their book; it also provides an essential tool to visualize and understand the connected void space that gives specific character to any city.

Like a diagram, the figure ground is exceptionally reductive in order to convey the complexities of urban space—public and private, solid and void, figure and ground, building and street. The reductive nature of the representation can be very valuable to communicate a concise idea about a city so that black and white clearly equal solid and void. But the city is rarely as crisp and clear-cut as a black and white representation of it. Because of the particular significance of the space of the street to the mass of the buildings, many figure grounds are better served when drawn near the ground (as seen in Giambattista Nolli's map of Rome). Unexpected volumes of space may be entirely ignored when translating an aerial view to a figure ground, or by using information generated from a geographic information system (GIS) viewer. The impact of the street level as the space of the city we move in and engage with is entirely lost in a figure ground that reveals only rooflines.

This kind of diagram can serve to illustrate the basic grain of the city, but cannot begin to illustrate the proportions of a city's specific space. For example, a defining characteristic of Milan, Italy, is the network of porticoes that run down many of the larger avenues of the city: these essential spaces to the city would be missing if only the mass at the roof level was shown. This space is part of the larger connected space of the city experienced when walking along the sidewalk. Examining two versions of the same figure ground of Milan you can see that the first (Figure 7.3) is cut as if the roof plane reflects the masses of the buildings, and the second (Figure 7.4) is cut near the ground to show the monumentality of the porticoed sidewalks. At the roof level, the car is clearly privileged over the sidewalk, but near the ground, the sidewalks are on the scale of the avenues they border, more accurately defining the space of this city. Philosopher Michel de Certeau, discussing the space of the city, describes this difference in view: "The ordinary practitioners of the city live 'down below,' below the thresholds at which visibility begins. ... they are walkers—*Wandersmänner*, whose bodies follow the thicks and thins of an urban 'text' they write without being able to read it."[8]

Another feature that can be overlooked or is typically flattened in a figure ground is the topography, because the essence of the drawing illustrates the immediate spatial relationships of the street and urban space. This immediacy is important to recognize experientially: if the topography is gentle, or the verticality of the masses of buildings in relation to the street are tight enough, you may not be able to perceive the topography shifting in a city. The "cut plane" of the figure ground typically moves with the landscape, slicing invisibly outward from your hip level as you walk through the city. In the case of more radical topography, the perception of the space of the city is dramatically altered if you can see beyond the buildings. Interestingly, Parma (the example shown

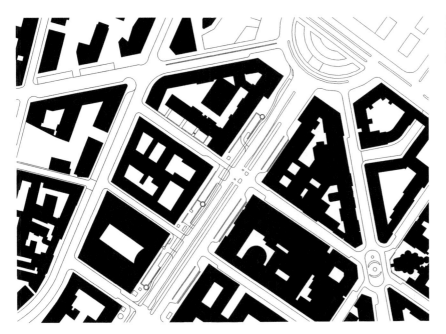

7.3
Figure ground of Milan,
Italy, cut at the level of
the roof.

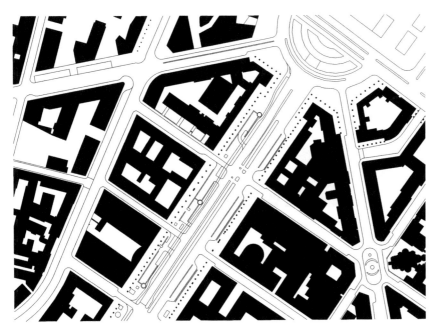

7.4
Figure ground of Milan,
Italy, cut at the level of
the street.

by Rowe and Koetter) is an Italian hill town where the landscape radically shifts through the city. Their argument is more strongly supported by showing a figure ground that does not illustrate this topography. By simply choosing to create a figure ground with a pure unmodulated cut plane, rather than an undulating one that collapses topography, a different character of the city is revealed.

7.5
Figure ground of Porto,
Portugal, cut with a
moving plane to
eliminate the topography.

Two versions of the same figure ground of Porto, Portugal, can give the sense of this idea. Porto is sited on the dramatically steep banks at the mouth of the Douro River as it flows into the Atlantic Ocean. The topography is such that you can feel contained within the street while simultaneously being able to see to the opposite side of the river and the city. While the sense of space in this area is similar to the traditional close-packed European city, you also experience the vast space of the entire river valley. The first figure ground (Figure 7.5) illustrates a moving cut plane of the Bairro da Sé neighborhood on the northern bank, one of the oldest and most dense areas of the city. The second (Figure 7.6) uses a flat cut plane where the buildings drop precipitously away, rendered in elevation to show the dramatic slope of the neighborhood and open space seen

at the street level. The topography of Porto is an extreme case, but for many younger cities the topography plays an equal role to the built fabric in creating the space felt at the street because these are in general not as dense.

At its most basic level, the figure ground can reduce an entire city to a single binary relationship. Because of these reductive qualities, the simultaneous perception of constrained and vast space can be seen individually, though both cannot be shown within the same drawing. There is, however, a certain amount of powerful elevational information provided within the white space of the ground, which offers an intriguingly grey area to the representation. These additive lines distinguish the figure ground from a simple diagram by biasing the white space of the street with more detail—the figure ground is also a plan of

7.6
Figure ground of Porto, Portugal, cut with a flat plane to reveal the topography.

Figure Ground

everything that exists beyond the buildings. The details added to a representation provide a potential depth to the reading of the space. For instance, most contemporary cities rely on an infrastructure of sidewalks and islands to assist with differentiating traffic flow, unless they are old enough to have been built to deal solely with the movement of humans and carts. This division of traffic flow is absolutely critical to how one perceives the space of the city, and a representation intended to communicate that space cannot ignore the hierarchy of movement through it. The line differentiating sidewalk and street also separates subtly different kinds of public space within the larger connected white space of the city.

The selection of what should be included in the white of the void or the black of the solid is a similar grey area in a figure ground—it is as much about solid and void as it is about the division between public space (as part of the city) and private space. In Giambattista Nolli's map of Rome, he deliberately renders the space inside the church white, equivalent to the street outside of it, implying that the church is as public as the street. From this reasoning, any number of transitional spaces can be considered part of the public realm and part of the white space of a figure ground, depending on how you choose to perceive the term public. These spaces might include front porches, balconies, retail space, alleys, and even the subway system's network of pedestrian pathways, to name a few. Choosing to indicate these in the black of the mass/private space or in the white/public space can entirely shift the intent of the representation. Robert Venturi, Denise Scott Brown, and Scott Izenour in their book *Learning from Las Vegas* take this idea to its limits by positing that if the church is a public space as seen in Nolli's map, then the casino lobbies on the Las Vegas Strip must also be considered public, as well as the parking lots: "A 'Nolli' Map of the Las Vegas Strip reveals and clarifies what is public and what is private, but here the scale is enlarged by the inclusion of the parking lot, and the solid-to-void ratio is reversed

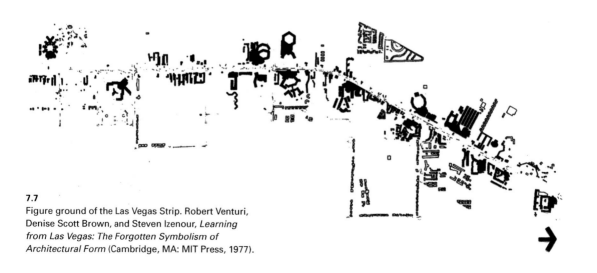

7.7
Figure ground of the Las Vegas Strip. Robert Venturi, Denise Scott Brown, and Steven Izenour, *Learning from Las Vegas: The Forgotten Symbolism of Architectural Form* (Cambridge, MA: MIT Press, 1977).

→

Spatializing Site

by the open spaces of the desert."[9] From the figure ground shown in Figure 7.7, they systematically reread the Strip to propose an entirely inverted sense of public and private space and upend the traditional notion of city.

It can be easy to see the manipulation of the features of a figure ground as a flippant game. Part of this is because the tool is simple—its simplicity allows for the clear reading of a city in a particular way, and it can frame how we perceive it. It is also a clear analytical tool that can proceed systematically once the rules are established, and the resultant drawing can either surprise or confirm what it is you already suspected. The city is in reality far more complex—created by hundreds, even millions of objects and individuals. What is extremely difficult to understand about the city is that you can only ever design components of it. Even master plans can only envision a piece of the larger organism of the city that will change over time. To an architect, the urban site cannot be understood with any one specific means of analysis, and any kind of representation can only hope to express an aspect of the city, frozen. The figure ground helps clarify or at the very least identify the substance which design can only help to define—its urban space.

Notes

1 The original map of Rome by Nolli is digitally available and discussed at great length at http://nolli.uoregon.edu.

2 This can be seen in many city maps available, particularly European sources such as the London A-Z, the British Ordnance Survey, etc.—color is often used in lieu of black and white.

3 Colin Rowe and Fred Koetter, *Collage City* (Cambridge, MA: MIT Press, 1979), 2.

4 Rowe and Koetter, *Collage City*, 38.

5 Rowe and Koetter, *Collage City*, 62.

6 Rowe and Koetter, *Collage City*, 58.

7 Rowe and Koetter, *Collage City*, 62–63.

8 Michel de Certeau, *Practice of Everyday Life*, trans. Steven Rendall. (Berkeley, CA: University of California Press, 1984), 93.

9 Robert Venturi, Denise Scott Brown and Steven Izenour, *Learning from Las Vegas: The Forgotten Symbolism of Architectural Form*, revised edition (Cambridge, MA: MIT Press, 1977), 19.

8

Comparative Analysis

Capturing the space of the city is inherently complex because many different objects work together to define it and not all of these objects are stationary. Buildings help frame urban space, but sidewalks, trees, and even the movement of people shape urban identity. It is what author Steven Johnson describes as driven by "micromotives" that "combine to form macrobehavior, a higher order that exists on the level of the city itself."[1] A complicated amalgam of bottom-up forces (individuals) and top-down forces (planners) give a city its individual character and its fabric. Because it is constantly a fusion of shifting parts, it can be difficult to rigidly define "Paris," "New York City," or "Rome," for instance. The borders change, the buildings change, the occupants change—it is almost easier to imagine that the city is reborn anew each day because the circumstances of every day would define it differently. While it might be a natural human predilection to categorize things, most people know a city through literature and images, or by living in or traveling through it, and they can probably tell you some defining characteristics. These defining characteristics would be very difficult to pick apart and pin down, but it is precisely the process of analyzing through comparison that is essential to designing for any urban context.

Comparison is the way we understand differences and similarities, how we identify things for what they are, and it is a way of recognizing patterns and exceptions. For example, consider a diagrammatic comparison of buildings and sites within a hypothetical city (Figure 8.1). We can identify three out of the four masses in the illustration as fairly similar, because they each attach to the same side; the fourth mass is distinct because it does not fit with the other three. There are many ways one could analyze this illustration, but two interpretations are worth discussing for the purposes of this chapter. The first is that all of the drawings

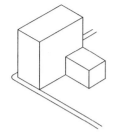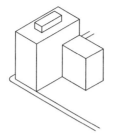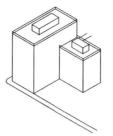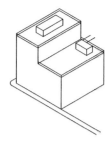

8.1
Comparison of building forms and sites.

shown in this comparison could be examples of an urban morphology or type within the city, such as L-shaped, where the fourth shows a distinct variation. Steven Holl, in his *Pamphlet 5: The Alphabetical City*, uses this method of comparison to explore various urban morphologies in New York City.[2] Another interpretation of this comparison is that they illustrate the evolution of one mass over time. A typical phasing diagram of a project on a site would be similar to this approach; it depends fundamentally on being able to see change from the initial drawing and read the initial drawing onto its variants. The drawings in this illustration would then be showing key moments of change where difference is apparent. Both interpretations give highly relevant information about a site and building based on its relationship to the context revealed through serial imagery. The interpretation depends on an articulated explanation to illuminate the comparison shown. For any given site this method of analyzing a comparison, or comparative analysis, can be a tool to recognize how to "fit" the context or not. Underneath this kind of analysis, there is also an implication about space—either spatial patterns within the city (the same "kind" of space that can be found in more than one place) or a specific space that has changed over time. The object of study in a comparative analysis is not inherently the "object" in an urban context.

There is a strong lineage of architects working to understand and characterize what a city *is*, analyzing both urban form and space through the medium of a specific city. Two examples from this lineage on urbanism merit study in relationship to each other because their methodologies are distinct but interrelated. In 1972, architects Robert Venturi, Denise Scott Brown and Steven Izenour wrote the seminal (and polemical) book *Learning from Las Vegas* to challenge the perception that urban fabric can only be found in older (European) cities: "Analysis of existing American urbanism is a socially desirable activity to the extent that it teaches us architects to be more understanding and less authoritarian in the plans we make for both inner-city renewal and new development."[3] The book is a sophisticated analysis of Las Vegas as a specific place (at a particular time in the 1970s—the city has changed a great deal since the book was written), but it is also a thesis on the more abstract idea of "city." Their goal was parity: analyzing and literally learning from Las Vegas, those lessons, regardless of the lowbrow associations the city has to gambling and overall kitsch, could be transferred to any city.

Dissecting the Las Vegas Strip through mapping and representation, the authors sought to take it apart in order to understand and define what they saw as a new and divergent kind of space.[4] The drawings in the book range from figure grounds to serial photography (similar in many respects to the photo books of Ed Ruscha)[5] to the diagrammatic overlays of dots and dashes inserted on a map of streets delineated as a series of lines. The theoretical space they observe in the city is discovered through the aggregation of all of the analysis illustrated in the book, and by looking specifically at the comparative analysis of speed and scale: "The commercial persuasion of roadside eclecticism provokes bold impact in the vast and complex setting of a new landscape of big spaces, high speeds, and complex programs."[6]

The comparative analysis of "directional space" (Figure 8.2) places the "space" of the city of Las Vegas into a pedigree of what might be considered more traditional urban spaces. Directional space requires movement through it, and it is defined by a system of communication as well as scale. The medieval street and eastern bazaar are compared with more American urban spatial systems such as Main Street and the shopping center. The drawing itself is highly reductive, working to compare radically different spaces by what they have in

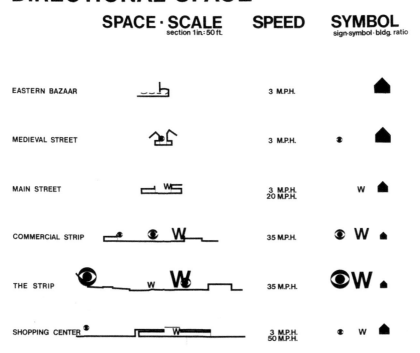

8.2
Directional space comparative analysis. Robert Venturi, Denise Scott Brown, and Steven Izenour, *Learning from Las Vegas: The Forgotten Symbolism of Architectural Form* (Cambridge, MA: MIT Press, 1977).

common—directionality created through movement, and the need to advertise for the purpose of attracting customers to sell products. The fact that the products sold are completely unrelated and the material qualities of the streets and buildings are different does not matter for the comparison—what matters is the size of the buildings relative to the street, the scale of the street itself, the scale of the signage needed to draw you to the products being sold, and the speed at which you may be moving through this system. Each section drawn is relative in scale to the next so that the proportions of the street can be compared. Adjacent to this is a list of the speed of movement associated with that space, as well as the ratio of sign to symbol to building. Each section is ranked by its speed, so the Las Vegas Strip is placed between the commercial strip and the shopping center. Two distinct variations are apparent through the comparison of the Strip: the signage is at a radically enlarged scale relative to the commercial strip and the building is entirely detached from its signage. Their analysis of the differences decodes a rationale for the space of the Strip:

8.3
Vast space comparative analysis, Las Vegas. Robert Venturi, Denise Scott Brown, and Steven Izenour, *Learning from Las Vegas: The Forgotten Symbolism of Architectural Form* (Cambridge, MA: MIT Press, 1977).

The vast parking lot is in the front, not at the rear, since it is a symbol as well as a convenience. The building is low because air conditioning demands low spaces, and merchandising techniques discourage second floors; its architecture is neutral because it can hardly be seen from the road.[7]

24. A comparative analysis of vast spaces

VAST SPACE

SPACE·SCALE
section, 1 in.=200 ft.

SYMBOL
symbol word architecture
$ W ▲ elements

VERSAILLES — statues-urns fountains partere curbs

ENGLISH GARDEN — trees ruins temples of love

BROADACRE CITY LEVITTOWN — usonian houses ranch houses

VILLE RADIEUSE — proto-megastructures

HIGHWAY INTERCHANGE — W green signs

THE STRIP — W ▲ see other topics

SPACE·SCALE·SPEED·SYMBOL

Spatializing Site

The next comparative analysis centers on the parking lot as a key feature of this particularly American space. "Vast space" (Figure 8.3), similar to the directional space analysis, seeks to relate the newly recognized space of the Strip to a larger history of vast spaces, such as Versailles. Using the same language of reductive sections, the space of Versailles, the English garden, Broadacre City, Ville Radieuse, and the highway interchange are compared with that of the Strip. Symbols, signs and buildings are again shown in ratio to each other, adding elements and photographs to the analysis. There is, of course, an undeniable irreverence in comparing Versailles to a highway interchange,[8] but again, the analysis looks specifically at spaces that are considered vast, regardless of certain features of the cultural context associated with them. It forces you to consider the idea that a grand palace and the Strip are actually comparable if the parameters of that comparison can be reduced to spatial considerations relative to the buildings, elements and attractors (symbols and signs that provoke movement) in that space. This new and simultaneously directional and vast space is a way of characterizing what Las Vegas *is*, but it is also meant to provoke thinking about the American city as a whole. By placing it into a history of ideal or utopian spaces they value it, looking beyond the asphalt and ostentatious signage (even if this is very much a part of what Las Vegas is) to learn about why it was created and imagine transferring that design knowledge to an entirely different setting.

Momoyo Kaijima, Junzo Kuroda, and Yoshiharu Tsukamoto had similar aspirations to Venturi, Scott Brown, and Izenour. Kaijima *et al.* even make reference to the *Learning from Las Vegas* authors in their introduction to the "guide book" they created in 2001 entitled *Made in Tokyo*. For the authors, *Learning from Las Vegas* "realised the power of placing 'bad architecture' within the line of architectural history."[9] Capitalizing on this idea of elevating "bad" architecture, they sought out the pervasive odd or hybrid combinations of commingling programs they describe as "*da-me*" ("no-good") architecture within the city, to re-map and characterize Tokyo. They constructed an elaborate cataloging system to place these pieces of urban fabric in relationship to each other based on their hybrid natures. Orders – Category, Structure, and Use[10]—define each "environmental unit" (so-called because "architecture" cannot be used to describe these buildings specifically, nor can "building"). If the programs of each of these units share an order it is considered "on", and if they do not, the order is "off". In this manner they group radically different buildings together, so that the entire system of commingling creates the urban fabric of Tokyo.

Each environmental unit is strictly represented through four repeating methods—locational plan, axonometric, verbal description, and photograph—following the template of a guidebook. For example, the Graveyard Tunnel and the Shrine Building are both located in the context of Tokyo by a site plan (Figures 8.4 and 8.5), depicting the location as a black solid within a small fragment of the city outlined in a postage-stamp-sized frame. Below the locational plan, a barebones

8.4
Location plan of the
Graveyard Tunnel, Tokyo.
Momoyo Kaijima, Junzo
Kuroda, and Yoshiharu
Tsukamoto, *Made in
Tokyo: Guide Book*
(Tokyo: Kajima Institute
Publishing, 2001).

8.5
Location plan of the
Shrine Building, Tokyo.
Momoyo Kaijima, Junzo
Kuroda, and Yoshiharu
Tsukamoto, *Made in
Tokyo: Guide Book*
(Tokyo: Kajima Institute
Publishing, 2001).

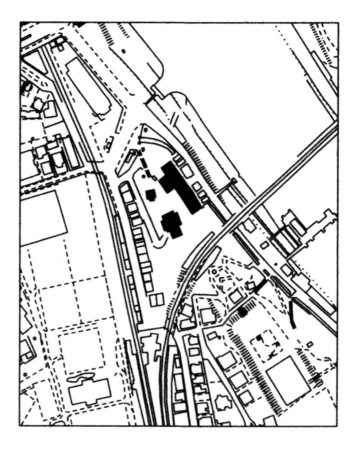

axonometric of the environmental unit is the focal point of every spread where constituent elements are labeled. These sparing labels (along with a brief bulleted verbal description) provide the only detail. The Graveyard Tunnel specifies the "tree," "car," "temple," "tunnel," and "graveyard," and its function is merely "graveyard + road" (Figure 8.6).[11] The drawing's principal purpose is to illustrate (in as few lines as possible) how a graveyard can also serve as an overpass in the context of the city. The Shrine Building shows the "sacred approach," leading to the top of a building of "apartments" and "shops/offices" (Figure 8.7). A "car" parks on this surface that is both shrine and roof.

On the neighboring page of each spread, a black and white photograph serves to elaborate the axonometric, locational plan and description, giving us evidence of its existence in the city. The Graveyard Tunnel and the Shrine Building

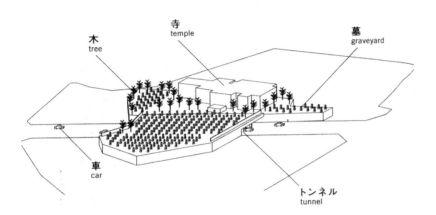

8.6
Axonometric diagram of the Graveyard Tunnel, Tokyo. Momoyo Kaijima, Junzo Kuroda, and Yoshiharu Tsukamoto, *Made in Tokyo: Guide Book* (Tokyo: Kajima Institute Publishing, 2001).

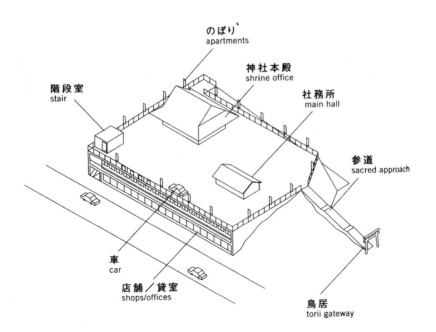

8.7
Axonometric diagram of the Shrine Building. Momoyo Kaijima, Junzo Kuroda, and Yoshiharu Tsukamoto, *Made in Tokyo: Guide Book* (Tokyo: Kajima Institute Publishing, 2001).

are entirely dissimilar, and they offer radically different hybridizations, but in the book they are equally categorized as "off–on–off," according to the authors' Orders.[12] These units do not share Category (landscape and road, religious place and office building), they do share Structure (both of these units are stacked vertically, conjoining their load-bearing structure), and they do not share Use (you do not drive on a highway in a graveyard or pray in a shrine and work in an office simultaneously). They are related by the system created by Kaijima, Kuroda and Tuskamoto; they may not be common hybridizations in Tokyo, but the type "off–on–off" is very common in the city, and this pervasive type helps to create the city:

> When we say that we can sense the pulse of Tokyo in the "da-me architecture" which includes some aspect of being "off", it means that even though the urban space of this city appears to be chaotic, in exchange, it contains a quality of freedom for production … We hope in our design work to clearly represent possibilities for the urban future by being consistent with the principle findings of our research.[13]

Like *Learning from Las Vegas*, *Made in Tokyo* is an attempt to understand the specific space of the city through comparison. However, *Made in Tokyo* is not trying to distinguish one city's space from a specific list of other spaces—it is an effort to construct similarities and see patterns in the city that may be difficult to describe as related.

Both books are looking at what on the surface appears to be radically unrelated things (Versailles and a highway interchange; Graveyard Tunnel and Shrine Building), but the analysis is about constructing the relationship between these things: it begins with the drawing—the drawing reduces each thing to what is relatable. The representations they use rely on repetition and variation, and the representational method deployed can exist at either end of the analysis, driving the outcomes generated or as a visualization of discoveries made through other means. For *Learning from Las Vegas*, the sectional diagrams at relative scales are the key, decoding the buildings relative to the signs and symbols in that space. For *Made in Tokyo*, the locational plans at relative scales help to place the reductive axonometrics back into the city. Each comparative analysis relies on the narrative provided to construct and articulate the comparison, which is embedded in the cohesive nature of publishing a book on both analytical projects. Comparative analysis can be considered a method deployed within both of these precedents as well as a method for constructing the entire project. *Learning from Las Vegas* and *Made in Tokyo* are a study of a city, bound together by the combination of both text (specific interpretation) and imagery (photo-graphic and drawn representation). The representations are individually diagrammatic, but through accumulation they are more than the sum of their constituent parts.

Each precedent delivers a strong thesis about its city of study because the architects who created it are pursuing a way to translate their research back into design. A single sectional diagram or reductive axonometric from either book can stand alone but would offer little for you to understand the complex nature of the city, and the drawing would read as an isolated object. Comparative analysis originates from the need to interpret a site in relationship to the things around it. It generates a perceived order from the complex and changing idea of the city that depends on specific subjective translation, reflecting the way in which the city itself is made, as a collection of many constructed objects put together to create a fabric defined by individual interpretations and conceptions of that fabric.

Notes

1   Steven Johnson, *Emergence: The Connected Lives of Ants, Brains, Cities and Software* (New York: Scribner, 2001), 90.

2   Steven Holl, *Pamphlet Architecture 5: The Alphabetical City* (New York: Pamphlet Architecture and William Stout Architectural Books, 1980).

3   Robert Venturi, Denise Scott Brown, and Steven Izenour, *Learning from Las Vegas: The Forgotten Symbolism of Architectural Form*, revised edition (Cambridge. MA: MIT Press, 1977), 6.

4   Venturi *et al.*, *Learning from Las Vegas*, 3–33.

5   Specifically, Ruscha's self-published photo books such as *Every Building on the Sunset Strip* (1966) or *Twentysix Gasoline Stations* (1936).

6   Venturi *et al.*, *Learning from Las Vegas*, 8.

7   Venturi *et al.*, *Learning from Las Vegas*, 9.

8   It is referred to as an "evolution of vast space" in Venturi *et al.*, *Learning from Las Vegas*, 13.

9   Momoyo Kaijima, Junzo Kuroda, and Yoshiharu Tsukamoto, *Made in Tokyo* (Tokyo: Kajima Institute Publishing, 2001), 11.

10 Kaijima *et al.*, *Made in Tokyo*, 14–15.

11 Kaijima *et al.*, *Made in Tokyo*, 104.

12 Kaijima *et al.*, *Made in Tokyo*, 16–17.

13 Kaijima *et al.*, *Made in Tokyo*, 14–15.

9.1
View of the street before construction, O'Donnell + Tuomey, Photographer's Gallery, London, UK, 2012.

9.2
Rendering of the gallery from the street, O'Donnell + Tuomey, Photographer's Gallery, London, UK, 2012.

9

Case Study
Photographer's Gallery—London, UK

The Soho district of central London, established in the 1600s with a past extending well beyond this, is steeped with the history of its own built fabric and the impact this small area has had on the world. It is bordered in the east by Charing Cross Road, the west by Regent Street, the south by Leicester Square and Coventry Street, and by Oxford Street in the north (Figure 9.3).[1]

The Photographer's Gallery, located in this district, is a large public gallery devoted to photography that has its own history in the area: it began life in 1971

9.3
Site diagram of the Soho district, London.

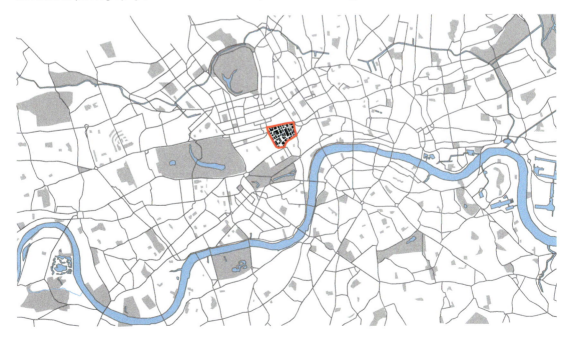

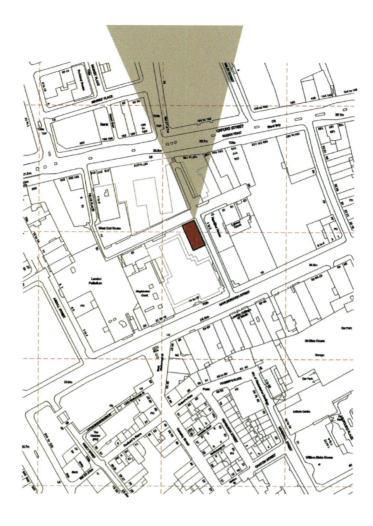

on Great Newport Street as the first independent gallery of photography in Britain. After their initial expansion into a neighboring building to accommodate increasing space requirements, the Gallery made the decision to move into an older Victorian brick warehouse building on Ramillies Street, just south of the major shopping area along Oxford Street (Figure 9.4).[2] The Irish firm of O'Donnell + Tuomey were brought in to re-envision the space in 2007. The existing warehouse, like most of the buildings in the area, was five stories tall with a piano nobile of stone on the ground floor topped by a three-story brick façade and a dormered roof above a cornice line of brick. A steel-framed structure holds up the brick and stone skin. The typical character of the buildings in the area is brick and steel construction with shared party walls, extending from four to eight stories. At the ground level, nearly all of Soho today consists of shops, restaurants, or small offices, while the floors above are typically housing.

The buildings that make up the district are constructed on an incredibly tightly packed and shifting grid of narrow street widths with almost complete frontage at the street; this fabric is only interrupted by narrower blind alleys and occasional throughways—passages that cannot accommodate cars and frequently do not go through entire blocks. The fabric is both contained and delineated by the larger avenues that border the district; Oxford Street, the northern border, can be seen on the location plan for the gallery. The viewing triangle on this plan highlights the narrow throughway off of Oxford Street that leads directly to the gallery, which was a primary focus for the overall design. Historically, as the city grew, tenement housing and poor living conditions persisted well into the 1800s in Soho. Because of its density and poor infrastructure, this area became the infamous location for a deadly outbreak of cholera in 1864, associated with the Broadwick Street pump (south of the gallery), which physician John Snow used to prove his theory that cholera is waterborne.[3] Evidence of Soho's grittier past remains today in the local pub named for Snow, as well as the sex shops and active late nightlife found in the area.

The character of the fabric is critical to understanding the nature of the transformation the warehouse at Ramillies Street underwent through the design by O'Donnell + Tuomey. John Tuomey defines their process as "thinking like archeologists might do, metaphorically prodding the ground, searching for traces of what made it the way it was, and sifting to unearth clues to inspire further transformation."[4] The gallery takes advantage of the warehouse structure on the site by building two additional stories on the original steel frame structure and reconfiguring the brick façade so that the addition and existing building could read as a whole. The exterior mass and skin, seen from your approach to the building, was of substantial importance to the architects, and their scheme relies on understanding, in many respects, the building that existed before its transformation. The façade of the upper two stories is made of black render, which is a kind of exterior plaster similar to stucco. The architects worked to integrate the addition by choosing not to extend the existing brickwork; instead, they integrated new and old by pulling the black render façade down over portions of the original brickwork, which, because the render sits in front of the original façade, gives the impression that the building may be entirely brick. The effect appears geological; similar to a ridge face made visible through tectonic action, the historical layers of the older fabric appear to be more visible by reading as if they have torn through the newer façade (seen in the model shown in Figure 9.5). John Tuomey describes this aspect of the project as "the day that Oxford Street cracked ... what happened when London's tectonic plates shifted and this great geological rift appeared".[5] This idea is also captured in their sketch of the project—the façade performs the same action that the narrow throughway does from Oxford Street, revealing the history through a crack in the fabric.

This "geological rift" plays a role not only in the massing of the overall building, but specifically in the way the openings in the façade have been restructured. The original building (Figure 9.7), as a steel frame structure with a brick façade, maintains a consistent aperture size for the upper three stories. All

9.6
Sketch of view from
Oxford Street, O'Donnell
+ Tuomey, Photog-
rapher's Gallery, London,
UK, 2012.

of the openings are inset behind the brick and stone; the ground floor façade also maintains inset windows of a repeating size. This gives the whole façade a sense of rhythm that is echoed throughout Soho and London. The elevation of the new building (Figure 9.8) creates an opportunity to alter the existing rhythm of this fabric by introducing oversized picture windows that run against the grain of repeated openings on the street. Sitting slightly outboard of the façade, these new windows (Figure 9.9) carve out small interior spaces to view the city. As architect John Tuomey describes it, these restructured windows create "little niches and viewing points that punctuate the purity of the container, moments of relief to refresh your concentration."[6] The disruption in the pattern of the existing façade does as much to draw attention to the pattern as it does to its exceptions. Inside the galleries, these windows can almost be mistaken for a piece of art on the wall. While the gallery itself contains photographic prints, the large picture windows literally frame the urban context as an alternative photograph, becoming a part of the gallery. The apertures' resemblance to large photographs persists on the exterior due to the reflectivity of the glass, reflecting back the city to its inhabitants.

9.7 Existing north elevation, O'Donnell + Tuomey, Photographer's Gallery, London, UK, 2012.

9.8 Proposed north elevation, O'Donnell + Tuomey, Photographer's Gallery, London, UK, 2012.

9.9 View out to the street from the galleries, O'Donnell + Tuomey, Photographer's Gallery, London, UK, 2012.

9.10 View from the street, O'Donnell + Tuomey, Photographer's Gallery, London, UK, 2012.

Case Study: Photographer's Gallery—London, UK

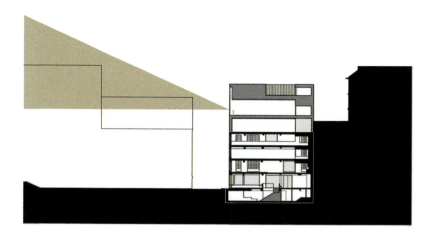

9.11
Section, O'Donnell +
Tuomey, Photographer's
Gallery, London, UK,
2012.

On the ground floor (seen in Figure 9.10), the rhythm of the façade is broken by a large horizontal expanse of glass, making the building appear as though the load-bearing corner has been cut away to expose the ground floor retail space. This window has a dramatic impact on the relationship of the building to the street: the expansive aperture captures the activities inside for passersby, as well as pulling the circulation of pedestrians off the street into the space. The strength of the design lies in how it works to integrate with the urban fabric and the program. Using the visible history embedded in the surrounding fabric as well as the nature of the photograph to seize a moment in time, the transformation of the existing building becomes the revelation of its history and the perpetual capturing of its present use. By exploiting the existing structure, the building is embedded in the existing fabric and subject to that structure's limits. The transformation of

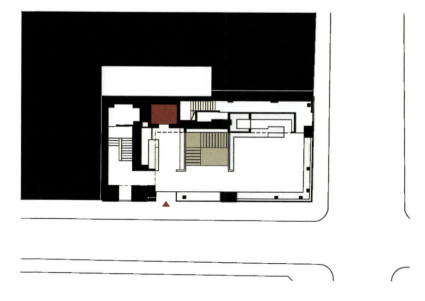

9.12
Ground floor plan,
O'Donnell + Tuomey,
Photographer's Gallery,
London, UK, 2012.

the façade masks the two-story addition on the original warehouse, but continues to work within the height range and depth of the surrounding buildings. Exposing the original brickwork in a way that interplays with the new fenestration and design allows the old and new to coexist in a state of equilibrium.

The project inherently performs in a similar manner to photography to capture time.[7] The play of time visible on the façade—seeing the passage of time in the weathering of materials and the transient moments caught through windows and reflections—is deeply intertwined with a larger transformative narrative that begins at the street level. The newly designed windows catch your eye as you walk down the street, cutting against the existing fenestration pattern of the neighboring buildings. You enter by crossing into the largest of these apertures at the ground; through a newly hollowed out opening in the ceiling, a staircase delivers you into the gallery spaces above. In the galleries, the same windows that drew you into the building now draw your eye back to the street as you walk through the photography on display. These windows are distinct from the typical façade—they literally invite you into them—they are niches created by design to return you to the street. The tectonic shift described by John Tuomey is apt: by shifting the urban fabric, the façade opens rifts and creates ridges, and a new and occupiable vertical urban terrain is created between interior and exterior, new and old.

Notes

1   F. H. W. Sheppard (ed.), "Estate and Parish History," in *Survey of London, volumes 33–34: St Anne Soho* (1966): 20–26, www.british-history.ac.uk/report.aspx?compid=41023.

2   Photographer's Gallery, "Infosheet: History and Building Information," http://thephotographersgallery.org.uk/images/Building_Infosheet_1__524d96fc4cf85.pdf.

3   Steven Johnson, *The Ghost Map: The Story of London's Most Terrifying Epidemic—and How It Changed Science, Cities and the Modern World* (New York: Riverhead Books, 2006).

4   John Tuomey, *Architecture, Craft and Culture: Reflections on the Work of O'Donnell +Tuomey*, Edge Series—Ideas on Art and Architecture (Cork: Gandon Editions, 2004), 41.

5   Oliver Wainwright, "The Photographer's Gallery by O'Donnell & Tuomey," www.bdonline.co.uk/the-photographers-gallery-by-odonnell-and-tuomey/5037081.article.

6   Wainwright, "The Photographer's Gallery."

7   This is similar to the tradition of street photography extending back to Eugene Atget, Walker Evans, and Robert Frank, where the photograph is as much a portrait of the city as a medium with which to capture the human condition. For more on the history of street photography, see: Colin Westerbeck and Joel Meyerowitz, *Bystander: A History of Street Photography* (Boston, MA: Little, Brown and Company, 2001).

Part IV

Systematizing Site

Any site is inherently complex, but it contains an underlying order driven by systems. While intricate and lengthy mathematical equations could attempt to more precisely describe this order, anything that we designate as a site is by its own nature already a design that is working to change its context. Predictive modeling of complex and dynamic behavior can help to legitimize or strengthen our understanding, but it is also essential to have a firm intuitive grasp of how this dynamic behavior works. A system, for the purposes of this book, encompasses everything and anything that persists beyond the boundaries of a site, or that can be tapped into, but it must also be mentally or literally able to be assembled into relatable parts.

The larger umbrella of systems as it relates to site is intended to push the limit of what a "site" conceivably defines. For example, to say a project is sited adjacent to a stream contains the "stream" within the scale of the project. That stream is much larger than its proximity to the project, and calling it simply a stream does not get at a larger understanding of the cycle of precipitation, flooding, or its relationship to a much larger system of surface water that makes the stream exist. Without drowning in a much deeper knowledge of hydrology, a designer must be able to understand the aspects of a site that will impact a design (such as flooding) and consider the inverse: what a design will do to a site (such as leaching chemicals or generating energy).

10

Flow

Flow, an applicable term in many scientific fields, can be used to describe any dynamic and fluid system. As it relates to understanding a site, the concept of flow is particularly relevant to natural forces, such as wind, water, and time, and to the forces of movement and trajectories of people or objects in space. These forces, because of their dynamic nature, are difficult to precisely articulate in the static world of representation, but their impact can be overwhelming and even life-threatening.

Many of the traditional diagrams students and architects use to consider complex and dynamic forces fail to conceptualize the total impact these forces have on a site. The diagram of the sun's path, the yearly precipitation, or a wind rose, for example (Figure 10.1), can be extremely useful to an architect who can effectively read and apply the information contained in them to conceptually situate that data in a site, but these kinds of diagrams only provide a fraction of the information needed to understand what may actually occur on site. They require a refined synthesis of the information provided in them, as well as intermediate steps between information, analysis, and design.

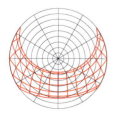  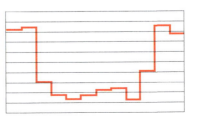

10.1
Sun path diagram [left]; wind rose diagram [middle]; annual average precipitation chart [right].

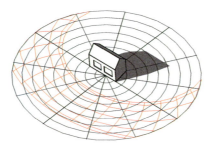 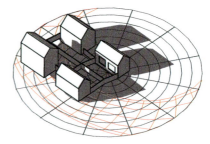

For instance, consider a sun path diagram of a site (Figure 10.2): it can hypo-
thetically inform you of a building's orientation to receive winter sun. What it will not
tell you is that the surrounding buildings or topography may cast a shadow on or
reflect light on your site, or that the mass of your building could also be contributing
to the overall complexity of the flow of light. The diagram of the sun path itself will
not visualize the specific idiosyncrasies of an individual site. The growing world of
computational modeling has enabled architects to more precisely envision many of
these forces in an accurate "real-time" manner, but these programs measure cause
and effect, removing the architect's capability to conceptualize the problem so that
a response can be designed based on the representation of the problem.

The methods demonstrated within this chapter will consider drawing the
forces of flow as a tool for conceptualization firmly in the hand of the architect.
This is not to undermine the tools available to architects to study these complex
systems, but rather to look at the way architects create the representation of a
dynamic system as a bridge to design. While noticeably dissimilar, the representations can be understood as a type, and there are patterns in the way they are
produced. The architects that will frame this chapter have designed systems to
understand flow that are diagrammatic in that they are an abstraction of what is
essentially an invisible and ephemeral force, while relying on a more sophisticated
language than the immediate communication of a diagram. These analytical
drawings attempt to understand the conditions of flow (existing and set in motion
by a design) through the process of drawing. They notate an elaborate scenario
that must be read from the drawing, in the way a map, a piece of music or dance
steps must be "read." Intriguingly, this type of analytical drawing can frame a
"before and after" (showing change over time or by defining a "problem" and
showing a change through design) using the same notational system.

The predominant dilemma of understanding complex real-life forces within a
two-dimensional static space is that a single representation cannot illustrate the flow
or passing of time. Similar to the process of storyboarding a motion picture or the
layout of comic strips, many architects have learned to bypass this problem by
considering a representation in sequence. Architect Sarah Wigglesworth, with
partner Jeremy Till, approaching the design of their house and practice at 10 Stock
Orchard Street, considered the conceptualization of the dining table the embodiment

of activity shared between house and work, the site which "retains the patina of time, the traces of past events indelibly etched into the surface."[1] By analyzing the process of eating a meal at the table, Wigglesworth built the conceptual foundation for translating this analysis to the site for her house and office.

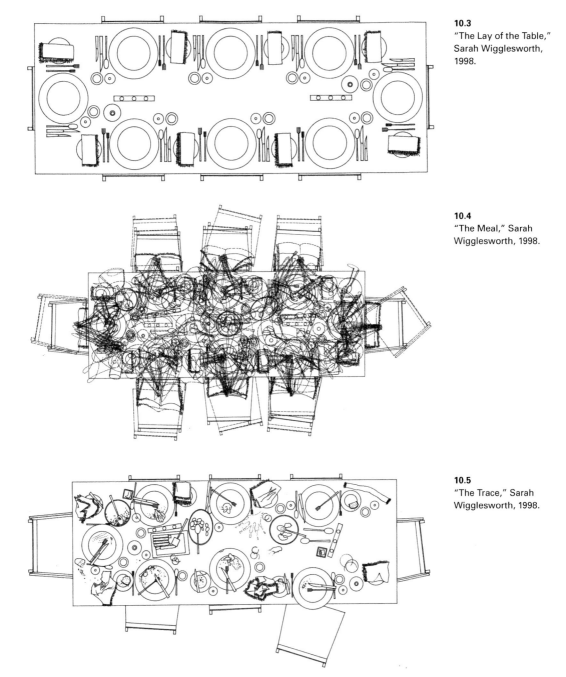

10.3
"The Lay of the Table," Sarah Wigglesworth, 1998.

10.4
"The Meal," Sarah Wigglesworth, 1998.

10.5
"The Trace," Sarah Wigglesworth, 1998.

In the sequence of three drawings—"The Lay of the Table," "The Meal," and "The Trace" (Figures 10.3–10.5)—movement and time are captured at two scales. The larger scale is that of the meal in its entirety, as a single repeated act within the course of the day. The second scale of movement and time exists within each drawing, using dashed lines to denote the position of things as they come to rest over the course of the drawing's timeframe, compressed into a single image. The analysis maps domestic use—the space in which we perform daily rituals. For Wigglesworth, "the Dining Table itself is the starting point for the project, acting as a trope for the design of spaces which inscribe home and work simultaneously."[2] While only one meal is represented in the analysis, any meal can be captured by the careful consideration of only one because it is a ritual of repeated activity. The process of the drawing relies on the author to synthesize many repetitions of the same process, eliminating any "false positives" or deviations from the standard (like a Thanksgiving feast would be to a typical meal). The analysis cannot be scientific in the same sense that a line graph with deviation markers would be: it is working at conceptualizing domestic patterns in a space.

The dining table is also a plan, and it has a sense of space that a line graph cannot have—it maps out trajectories and creates the spaces of least activity based on the parameters set by a chair, an arm, the physical dimensions of the table, and the plates. It also seeks to reveal the entropy inherent in living with objects. The system of representation in the drawings allows us to perceive the space created by the process of entropy, which Wigglesworth builds on to design the larger site plan for the house, accommodating the habitual nature of use observed at the dinner meal to the larger strategy for the project.

Creating a method of notating movement over time can also translate to a radically different scale and way of perceiving time. Louis I. Kahn, in his "Towards a Plan for Midtown Philadelphia," first published in *Perspecta* in 1953, was looking at the dilemma of the tight-knit and utopian grid of Center City, which occupies the original city designed and founded by William Penn.[3] Kahn developed a system of notation to analyze the traffic patterns within the existing gridded streets so that he could propose an alteration to the pattern that would change how the streets would be used and offer an opportunity for design. His notational system used five different symbols:[4] the first, dots in a line, denote "staccato" movement, indicating the sedate speed of a horse drawn wagon, carriage, or trolley. Arrows indicate "go" traffic—automobiles with a certain direction, bent on moving through the system. Three stationary symbols indicate the transition from go to staccato, from fast to slow (and from automobile to foot traffic): the cross denotes an intersection, the turning arrows indicate parking (the larger versions indicate a commercial garage or "wound up street"), and the large angle brackets denote municipal garages. The tick marks seen adjacent to the parking arrows and brackets indicate parking spaces. For Kahn, "The present mixture of staccato, through, stop and go traffic makes all the streets equally

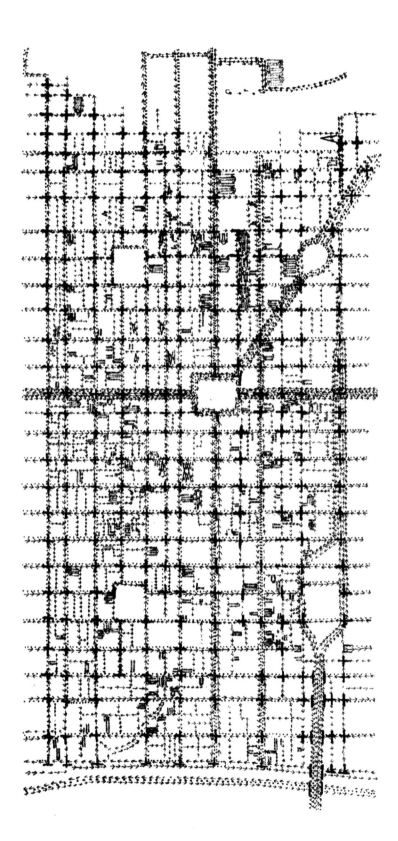

10.6
Existing movement
pattern, Louis I. Kahn,
Midtown Philadelphia
master plan,
Pennsylvania, USA, 1953.

Flow

10.7
Proposed movement
pattern, Louis I. Kahn,
Midtown Philadelphia
master plan,
Pennsylvania, USA, 1953.

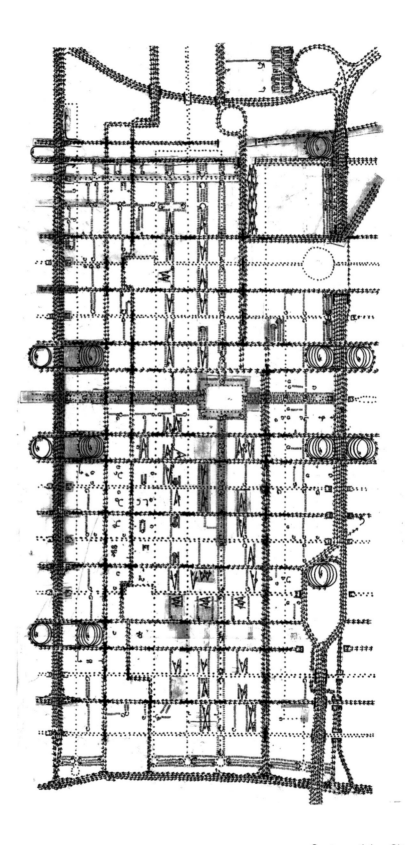

ineffectual."[5] Looking at the existing movement pattern (Figure 10.6), the number of crosses, indicating intersections, dominates the drawing, as well as a pervasive amount of parallel traffic at different speeds.

The notational system Kahn created centers on a concern for the sense of rhythm that the street currently has. By characterizing the speed of the traffic, he could illuminate the problem, and create the means to eliminate the problem. It was necessary "to re-define the use of streets and separate one type of movement from another so that cars, buses, trolleys, trucks and pedestrians will move and stop more freely, and not get in each other's way."[6]

Kahn's proposed solution alters the perceived cacophony of overlapping rhythms within the existing street grid through separation and hierarchy (Figure 10.7). He defines "through" streets around the perimeter of the Center City, which can be seen in his proposed solution as a large band of arrows that move around the perimeter indicating the lanes of traffic and the proposed expressway that would eventually be built. "Go" streets are created for quick-moving traffic through Center City, shown in his proposed solution as two parallel lines of arrows to indicate a one-way street with two lanes. Staccato or "stop" streets are designed for slower moving and stop-and-start traffic. Certain streets become entirely pedestrianized: "terminal" streets designated specifically for shopping.[7] These can be seen as streets denoted with a series of single dots, differentiated from staccato streets, which are denoted by parallel dots or tick marks that indicate parking. Many of the dark crosses from the existing movement pattern have been entirely eliminated or converted into a single dark line to show that stopping only occurs in one direction. He also implements an elaborate parking structure network that proposes new monumental tower-like garages that will pull people out of their cars and into the street, reusing the existing parking garages for service and unloading.

Kahn's proposal is determined by the way in which he initially conceptualizes the system of the flow of traffic. Again, the drawings are not meant to illustrate a specific moment in time, what might occur at rush hour, or an average of the amount of cars that actually travel through these streets. Both existing and proposed plans notate the patterns of movement on the site according to the rules created by the notational system, which is the summation of Kahn's experience with Center City. Whether or not his proposal coincides with current "best" solutions for creating a friendly pedestrian urban environment, the analysis and the proposed design are compelling because the representational system directly links the existing site to the design. The proposal is an analysis of future movement through the same site. The solution re-conceptualizes the street; while there are designed elements to his proposal, the overall plan redesigns the site, reordering the system of flow.

Moving beyond notation to the built translation of movement, Laurie Hawkinson and Henry Smith-Miller's project for the Land Port of Entry in Massena, New York, takes advantage of the existing notational system we take for granted that is literally painted on our streets. Smith-Miller and Hawkinson became very interested in the amount of time it takes to pass from one country to another, consuming a vast amount of space in the process. The 57-acre site of the project is both incredibly large and at the same time a single invisible line struck between one country and another. While any land port of entry will exist as a building and a gateway, the sequence of approach (and the design) begins long before you arrive at the gate. Similar to a tollbooth on a toll road, the architecture involved in allowing you to arrive successfully to pay your toll begins much earlier than when you may see the booth. Reyner Banham recognizes this phenomenon when discussing the highways of Los Angeles:

> ... the sign must be believed. No human eye at windscreen level can unravel the complexities of even a relatively simple intersection ... fast enough for a normal human brain moving forward at up to sixty mph to make the right decision in time, and there is no alternative to complete surrender of will to the instructions on the signs.[8]

10.8
Rendering of the proposed traffic lines, Smith-Miller + Hawkinson, Massena Land Port of Entry, New York, USA, 2009.

As a driver on the road, you are trained to understand the notational system that markings and signage provide for your safety and to create flow. In essence, the notational system creates what it represents. Every driver must buy into the system of markings (or pay the penalty) for the infrastructure of the highway to

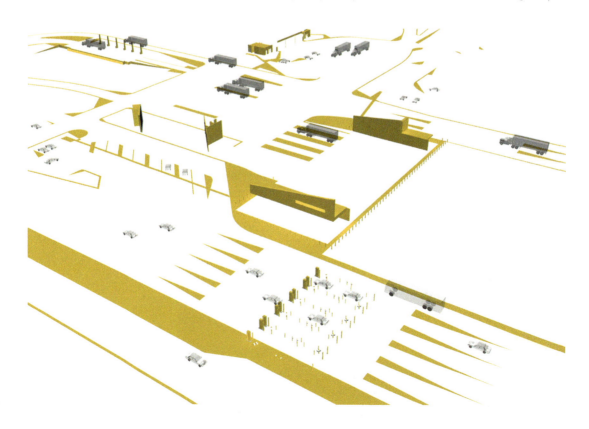

be activated. The architecture in place on any highway extends far beyond its buildings—it is in the notated instructions of the signs and markings on the road where the architecture unfolds.

For Smith-Miller and Hawkinson, analyzing the interaction between written and implicit signage on the road became the impetus for the design of the Land Port of Entry in Massena (Figure 10.8). The architects were seeking a way of organizing what can be quite a chaotic or disorienting experience. Road signs, lane changes, speed limits, checkpoints, and interviews are a small part of the entire process both people and goods go through to move over the border. Much like Banham's description, the "complete surrender" to signage on the road creates the opportunity to design the system that controls you—the signage itself. These signs are not simply the placards alongside the roadway: they are embedded in the asphalt through painted road surface markings.[9] By isolating the yellow markings needed for the site, Smith-Miller and Hawkinson's rendering exposes the architecture underpinning the project.

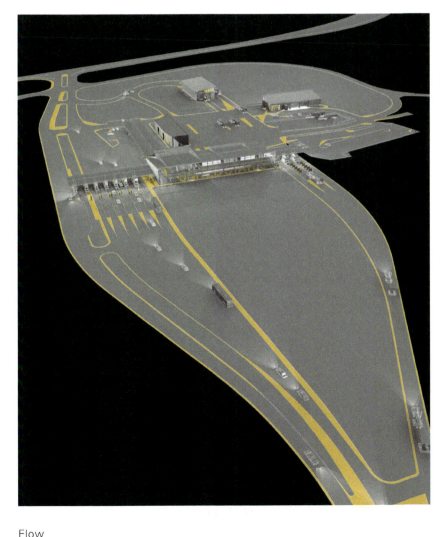

10.9
Rendering of the overall traffic flow, Smith-Miller + Hawkinson, Massena Land Port of Entry, New York, USA, 2009.

The design for the Land Port of Entry at Massena begins with the yellow-painted pavement markings already in place, capitalizing on the implicit knowledge of these markings so that the painted yellow surfaces take on a life of their own, notating any path of movement (Figure 10.9). The markings designed for the site delineate lanes, subtly distributing cars to inspection areas and trucks carrying goods off the main flow to a separate circulation system for goods. Each lane shift and channelizing device adds to the matrix of moving objects and people that must be coordinated through the site to ensure fluid interaction, exchange, and speed. Hatched safe zones demarcate walking areas, allowing pedestrians and employees to enter and exit their cars and move fluidly alongside traffic lanes. The paint defines the site, which is defined by movement systems designed to categorize, inspect, and allow passage.

While by no means comprehensive, the methods for considering movement and time introduced in this chapter all explicitly use the analysis and understanding of flow as the anchor and catalyst for the design. Movement and time are all programmatic needs, which led the designers to define the systems of flow in order to design for them. What is particularly relevant to these three projects is that the perceived invisible or intangible conditions of the site are represented so that the design can be created from the same system. The drawings are analytical in nature, but may not illustrate the actual process of analysis; instead, they show the larger itinerary of how things change and move on a site or in a space. By inventing or exploiting a system of representation that can portray the understanding of flow on a site, the design of the project shapes flow while remaining unbound to the physical and visual characteristics of the analysis (allowing the potential translation of the scale of the dining room to the scale of the site or the character of the arrow to shape the building).

Notes

1   Sarah Wigglesworth and Jeremy Till, "Table Manners," in *The Everyday and Architecture*, Architectural Design Profile no. 134, ed. Sarah Wigglesworth and Jeremy Till (London: Academy Editions, 1998), 31.

2   Wigglesworth and Till, "Table Manners," 31.

3   USHistory.org, "A Brief History of Philadelphia," www.ushistory.org/philadelphia/philadelphia.html.

4   Louis I. Kahn, "Toward a Plan for Midtown Philadelphia," *Perspecta*, vol. 2 (1953): 17.

5   Kahn, "Toward a Plan for Midtown," 11.

6   Kahn, "Toward a Plan for Midtown," 11.

7   Kahn, "Toward a Plan for Midtown," 11, 18.

8   Reyner Banham, *Los Angeles: The Architecture of Four Ecologies* (London: Penguin, 1971), 219.

9   For a detailed list of specific U.S. highway markings see two publications by the U.S. Department of Transportation's Federal Highway Administration: *Standard Highway Signs*, available at http://mutcd.fhwa.dot.gov/SHSe/Pavement.pdf, and *United States Pavement Markings*, available at http://mutcd.fhwa.dot.gov/services/publications/fhwaop02090/uspavementmarkings.pdf.

11

Infrastructural Networks

The dynamic forces on a site, from nature and from human habitation, often require systems built in response to these complex and often unpredictable flows. They are infrastructural systems, which control or channel the forces of flow and change, such as storm water management, electrical distribution, or street layout. Because these systems are much larger than a typical architectural project, they often fall under the purview of planners or independent authorities.

It is more complicated to understand the nature of infrastructure systems than the point at which they can be tapped into, in the sense that it is easier to know how to plug into an outlet than to understand all the wiring in a house. Often architects take for granted the infrastructure of a site without considering the vital role it plays in shaping a design, in the same way that not understanding the wiring in a house can lead to the house burning down or never having an outlet where you need one.

The projects introduced in this chapter, like the previous one, are both analysis and proposition, where the analysis frames and shapes the architecture, and can be seen as a return to the beginning of the book and the way a site is defined. They provoke a reimagining of what a site can be—its extents, definition, and meaning—and are intended to be roughly archetypal, or at least able to posit a pattern in approach at a scale much larger than might be typical for an architect to consider. The scale is significant to these projects as it forces an abstraction of what is more classically the scale of the design. Suddenly the design of the systems of a building can be translated to a global, national or regional scale. Like plumbing stacks and ductwork, there are rigid components at these scales that work with and manage dynamic forces to create a (hopefully) symbiotic relationship that is networked to even larger systems.

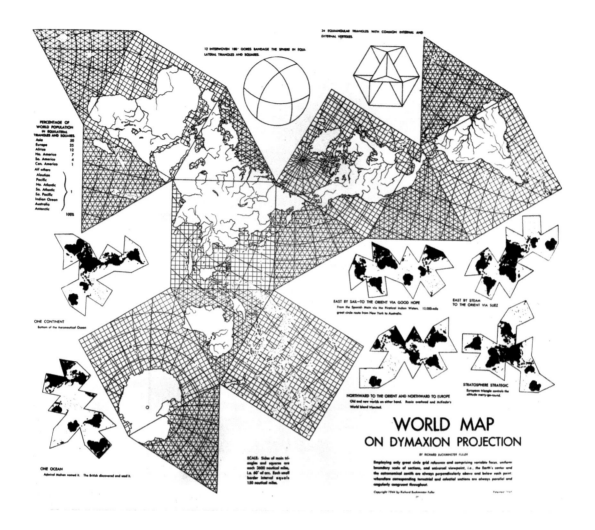

WORLD MAP
ON DYMAXION PROJECTION

BY RICHARD BUCKMINSTER FULLER

Employing only great circle grid reference and comprising variable focus, uniform boundary scale of sections, and universal viewpoint, i.e., the Earth's center and the astronomical zenith are always perpendicularly above and below each point; wherefore corresponding terrestrial and celestial sections are always parallel and angularly congruent throughout.

Copyright 1944 by Richard Buckminster Fuller

11.1
World map on Dymaxion projection, R. Buckminster Fuller, 1944.

Image courtesy of the Estate of R. Buckminster Fuller.

11.2
[Opposite] World Energy Map, R. Buckminster Fuller, 1960.

Image courtesy of the Estate of R. Buckminster Fuller.

R. Buckminster Fuller's series of Dymaxion maps, based on his patented "Dymaxion projection" system, is conceivably the broadest and most inclusive definition one could make for a site. Taking on the entire globe, Fuller worked out a system of projection that mapped the earth onto an icosahedron, evenly distributing the amount of distortion created through the process of projection (Figure 11.1). Most maps of the world we typically see project the surface of the globe, a sphere, onto a cylinder that can be sliced and unrolled.[1] Many of these maps work to reduce the amount of distortion created, but in principal this makes objects nearer the equator appear much smaller (like Africa) and objects closer to the poles much larger (like the United States) than they really are. Fuller's system of Dymaxion projection more evenly distributes the distortion created so that overall the continents are more in scale to each other. Because his system relies on unfolding a geometric volume, it can be outspread into different configurations, allowing us to perceive the world with alternative emphases. For

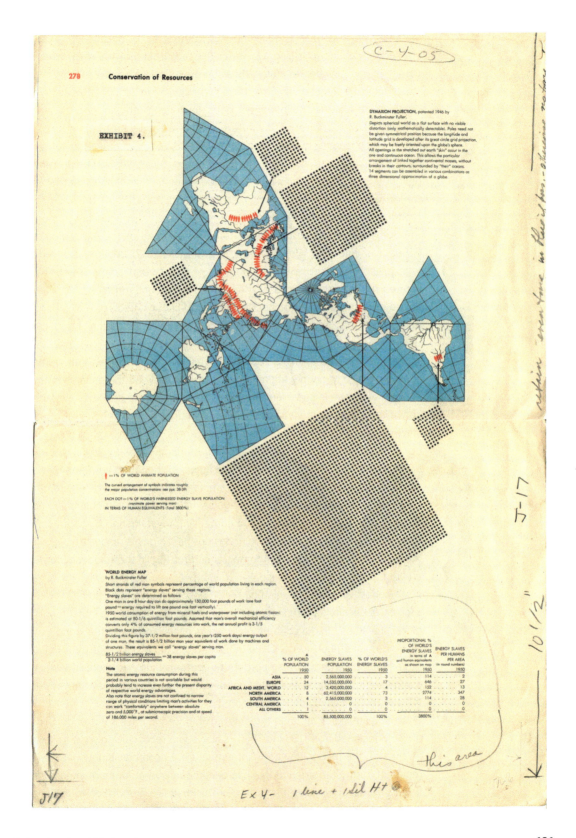

instance, we can unfold the world to capture it as all one ocean, or all one connected continent. It also allows for the recentering of the map, where any continent can take center stage and all others revolve around it.

Radically ahead of his time, Fuller, who has been described as an inventor, designer, educator, philosopher, poet and geometrician, was extremely concerned with sheltering the future world—a future that depended on the amount of space for human habitation, the number of resources to supply that habitation, and the conflicts that prevented those resources from being distributed.[2] By rationalizing available information on these global resources into the amount one human needs to survive and the amount that human can produce, he exposed the way that energy is distributed (inequitably) in the world through the translation of these figures onto a map of the earth as a single connected land. His World Energy Map (Figure 11.2) depicts little red men where each icon represents 1 percent of the "world animate population," located roughly at the lines of major population concentrations, as well as a series of dots that are attached to these populations, each of which depicts 1 percent of the "world's harnessed energy slave population"[3] and can be understood as the visualization of energy infrastructure.

Fuller defines a man's "energy slaves" as the machines that create the energy needed to supply the amount consumed beyond the estimated amount of work one man is capable of doing in a day. Using the statistics available, he converted these to a visualization of the distribution of the world's "energy slaves." The gross disparity of the United States' consumption of energy to its population can be easily seen relative to its neighbors—for Fuller, to achieve balance was to "populate the yurts and igloos of the world with energy slaves; freedom from want and freedom from fear are functions of environmental control."[4] While the actual facts and figures have changed demonstrably since he created this "site" analysis,[5] it is a compelling investigation that framed what became an entire Dymaxion world of designs based on his rationale for sheltering the future world through environmental control—from the geodesic domes he created to the Dymaxion house.

Robert W. Marks, writing on Fuller, describes this transition: "It was then a logical necessity for him to make the jump from shelter to the constituent parts of the universe."[6] In our contemporary world, visualizing the entire world's energy resources is difficult to conceive without political borders, but by framing the representation without these borders the potential infrastructure of distribution can be seen, and the entire world contained within the populated zones defines the site for his Dymaxion interventions.

At a smaller scale than the entire globe, Cedric Price's Potteries Thinkbelt project, designed from 1964 to 1966, is also about reconceiving what a site might be through the recognition of its infrastructure. Encompassing a relatively large region of north Staffordshire that had once been known for its manufacturing of pottery wares in England, the Potteries Thinkbelt is a proposition to revitalize an

Systematizing Site

area of which Price wrote: "As far as built physical environment goes it is a disaster area, largely unchanged and uncared for since the nineteenth century."[7] Price had grown interested in the idea of mobile education, and his proposal for the region offered an opportunity to create a new "industry" in education that could spawn more industry, keeping residents and building jobs. The program dictated the site for the project: north Staffordshire was ideal because of the density of the population, access to national transport, the existing state of advanced education in the area, and the need for revitalization and new industry. Price was uninterested in building a single campus hub for the region, and it would not work to serve the whole area by privileging the town in which it was built. Instead Price chose to build his proposal quite literally on the rails, out of the area's underutilized road and rail network: "The Thinkbelt takes advantage of the existing rail network and stations. The Madeley and Pitts Hill sections of the Thinkbelt rail net are surplus to British Rail's passenger carrying requirements and are due to be closed to passenger traffic."[8]

The overall plan showing the "primary road net" and "desire lines" is both a map of the region's roads and rail, as well as a carefully analyzed and selected network that would be needed to create the infrastructure for a continuous delivery system of mobile education that could exist over the entire region (Figure 11.3).

11.3
Overall plan showing primary road net and desire line, Cedric Price, Potteries Thinkbelt, north Staffordshire, England, 1964.

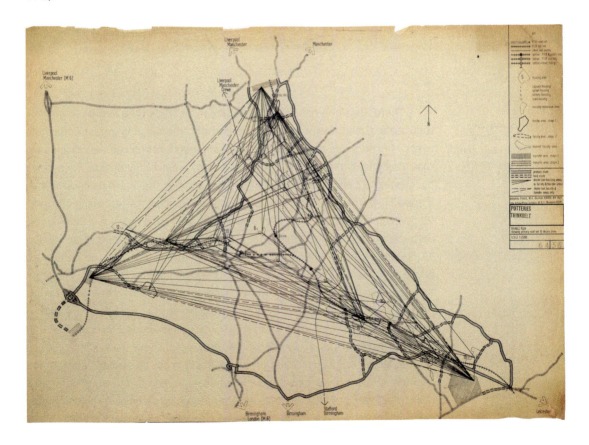

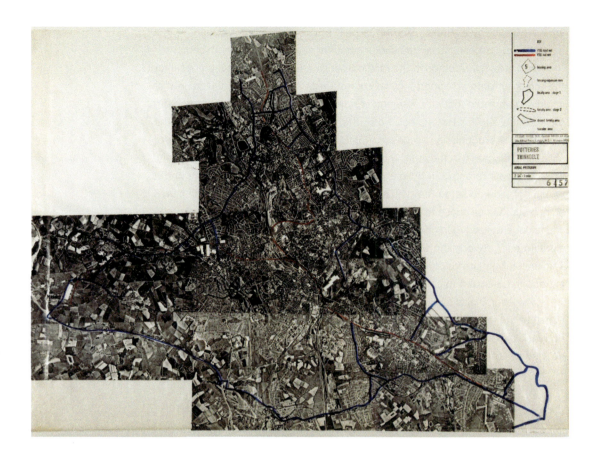

11.4
Plan of road and rail
network, Cedric Price,
Potteries Thinkbelt, north
Staffordshire, England,
1963–1966.

There are three principal transfer areas located in the largest towns that required a strong desire to go between them: the existing infrastructure that already linked these three cities enabled a network of repurposed rail lines and roads to connect the larger housing and faculty areas of the design. Price began by mapping out and selecting existing routes through the region on an aerial map (Figure 11.4). The scheme is created directly out of this tracery, carving out zones for housing and faculty. Train tracks and roads are coded by color, drawn directly onto the photograph to create the final plan. The final master diagram (Figure 11.5) depicts the existing context as grey zones for the "built up" areas and whole towns are reduced to single letters. Examining the key for this diagram, there are only four items that are "new" elements in the scheme—transfer areas, faculty areas, and two types of housing—implying that the reappropriation of existing elements is as important as the physically designed objects within the project. The site is essentially defined by the reconceiving of the systems in place. Price's design for the Thinkbelt project expands from the master diagram into each constituent part, from the distinct housing types to the transfer areas at each larger town, to the faculty areas where teaching takes place. Each of these elements plugs into the larger site to create a stable system at multiple scales.

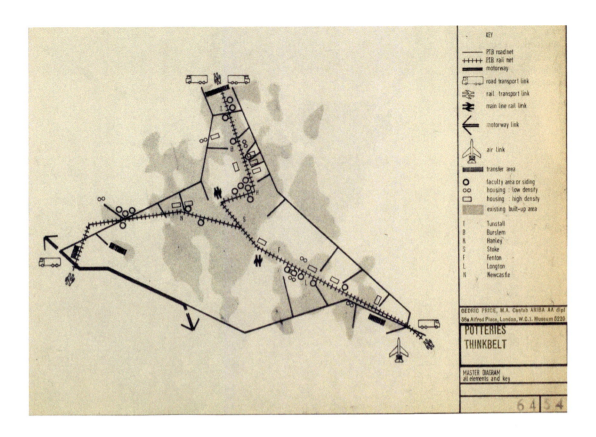

Inside the image (key):

KEY

PTB road net
PTB rail net
motorway
road transport link
rail. transport link
main line rail link
motorway link
air link
transfer area
faculty area or siding
housing : low density
housing : high density
existing built-up area

T   Tunstall
B   Burslem
H   Hanley
S   Stoke
F   Fenton
L   Longton
N   Newcastle

CEDRIC PRICE, M.A. Cantab ARIBA AA dipl
38a Alfred Place, London, W.C.1. Museum 5220

POTTERIES
THINKBELT

MASTER DIAGRAM
all elements and key

6.4 5.4

Lateral Office's work achieves similar ends to that of Fuller and Price by reconceiving the nature of a site, building on the definition of its infrastructure. Mason White, partner of Lateral Office, describes infrastructure as the locale for design: "Seemingly possessing properties of architecture, landscape, urban design, engineering, and planning, infrastructure has wedged itself into an ambiguous, yet powerful, position relative to the spatial disciplines, and, with that, relative to design, functionality, and expression."[9] Capitalizing on this ambiguity, their firm works specifically to create projects where the "future infrastructure lies in bundling multiple processes with spatial experiences."[10] Their project entitled "Water Ecologies/Economies," for the Salton Sea in California, looks at the potential to reinvent a "terminal" lake.[11] The lake's salinity is extremely high, because the valley was originally a seabed that was flooded by fresh water, which currently suffers from excessive irrigation runoff and high evaporation rates that allow the salts to accumulate. Their project attempts to recapture the fresh water and create different zones of industry, recreation, and protected habitats that could all work together to thrive off the sea (see Figure 11.6).

Water Ecologies/Economies begins by defining the lake as a multivalent resource. Like Price's Thinkbelt, there is more than one scale of activity that has been designed into the system, and the site fits the needs of the program by

11.5
Master diagram, Cedric Price, Potteries Thinkbelt, north Staffordshire, England, 1963–1966.

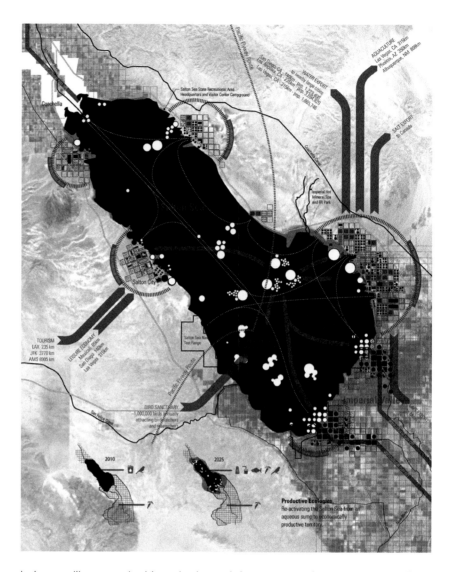

being readily networked into the larger infrastructure of water resource distribution in California. The master plan denotes five larger shoreline development areas that promote industry, recreation or remediation; like Price's desire lines, there are dashed lines and arrows to indicate the network of needed infrastructure to balance the system. These lines anticipate transportation and water infrastructure, as well as the migratory paths of the waterfowl attracted by newly created wetlands anticipate a needed biological "infrastructure." White circles float on the blacked out surface of the water, activating the sea as well as the shoreline in the larger design of the system.

At the next layer down (Figure 11.7), there emerges a kit of parts, similar to Price's faculty areas and housing (the key is now along the bottom of the drawing), where individual components are deployed as a kind of gridded quilt, creating the texture of development that grows out from the design of the

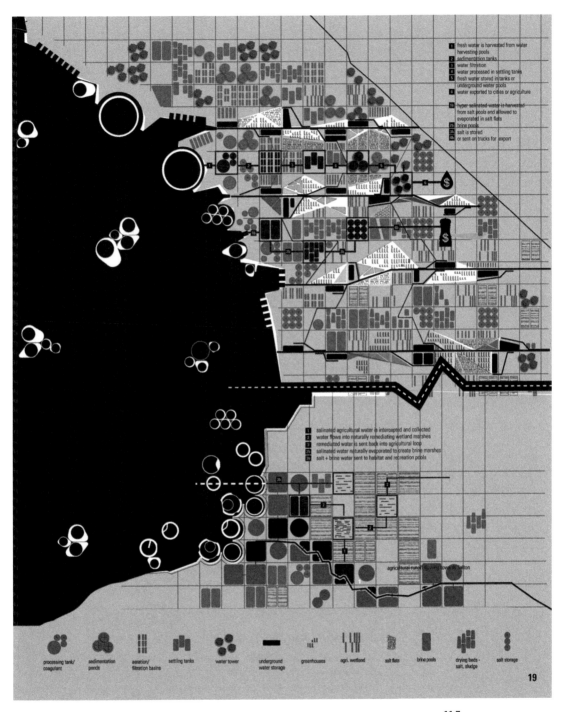

1 fresh water is harvested from water
  harvesting pools
2 sedimentation tanks
3 water filtration
4 water processed in settling tanks
5 fresh water stored in tanks or
  underground water pools
6 water exported to cities or agriculture

1b hyper salinated water is harvested
   from salt pools and allowed to
   evaporated in salt flats
2b brine pools
3b salt is stored
4b or sent on trucks for export

1 salinated agricultural water is intercepted and collected
2 water flows into naturally remediating wetland marshes
3 remediated water is sent back into agricultural loop
2b salinated water naturally evaporated to create brine marshes
3b salt + brine water sent to habitat and recreation pools

agricultural runoff flowing toward Salton

| processing tank/ coagulant | sedimentation ponds | aeration/ filtration basins | settling tanks | water tower | underground water storage | greenhouses | agri. wetland | salt flats | brine pools | drying beds - salt, sludge | salt storage |

19

infrastructure. Embedded in this plan are diagrammatic lines that link components, illuminating the processing of newly invented resources and their products, such as salt and money earned off the creation of water. While Price's Thinkbelt depends on its accessible population and the existing road and rail

11.7
Plan of the shoreline,
Lateral Office, Water
Ecologies/Economies,
Salton Sea, California,
USA, 2010.

infrastructure to catalyze the project-cum-process, Lateral Office's Salton Sea project depends on the reinvention of a "dead" environment to catalyze a recreational and industrial resource that will attract a future population to it.

All three of the projects introduced in this chapter share a goal to create a kind of designed closed loop system or ecology, sustained by recognizing all the factors that perpetuate the system. The term "ecology" seems apt for these projects because while each contains designed components that utilize infra-structure in a mechanical (read: predictable) way, they ultimately depend on the "natural" (read: unpredictable) forces of human consumption and the physical environment. This type of project aims at lofty programmatic goals: bringing education to a declining region of a country, equalizing the balance of energy production and consumption to the world, or bringing water to a region while also revitalizing a defunct natural resource. Interestingly, those programmatic goals produce and define the parameters of the site: the design is absolutely and inextricably linked to its site. You could, for instance, choose to bring education to another declining region in another country, but it would be a radically different proposal with different infrastructural networks, leading to an entirely distinct proposal. Without the program, the infrastructural needs are not apparent, but the infrastructure needed depends entirely on the specificities of the site.

As in the previous chapter, there are overlapping techniques used to represent the systems of the site, but distinct from the forces of flow, there are two types of notation introduced—what might be called conduits and a kit of parts. Conduits provide for flowing forces, such as rail or automobile traffic. A kit of parts describes the locationally static pieces of the analysis, overlapping with the design components added to this system. There is also a reconception required by all of these projects when looking at the site. Whether that is a recentering and unfolding of the map of the world, or the declaration that a terminal lake is instead life supporting, the alteration of perception is critical to the re-presentation of the site.

Notes

1   For a more expansive introduction to the different projection systems used in world mapping, see Arthur Howard Robinson, *Which Map is Best? Projections for World Maps* (Falls Church, VA: American Congress on Surveying and Mapping, 1986).

2   R. Buckminster Fuller, "We Call it Earth," in his *Nine Chains to the Moon* (Carbondale, IL: Southern Illinois University Press and Feffer & Simons, 1938), 50–61.

3   Text from the world energy map: "'Energy slaves' are determined as follows: One man in one 8 hour day can do approximately 150,000 foot pounds of work (one foot pound = energy required to lift one pound one foot vertically. 1950 world consumption of energy from mineral fuels and waterpower (not including atomic fission) converts only 4% of consumed energy resources into work, the net annual profit is $3\frac{1}{5}$ quintillion foot pounds. Dividing this figure by $37\frac{1}{2}$ million foot pounds, one year's (250 work days) energy output of one man, the result is $85\frac{1}{2}$ billion man year equivalents of work done by machines and structures. These equivalents we call 'energy slaves' serving man."

4   Robert W. Marks, *The Dymaxion World of Buckminster Fuller* (New York: Reinhold Publishing Corporation, 1960), 53.

5   A compelling project based on similar information gathering can be seen in the work of MVRDV shown in Winy Maas/MVRDV, *Metacity/Datatown* (Rotterdam: MVRDV/010 Publishers, 1999).

6   Marks, *The Dymaxion World*, 20.

7   Cedric Price, "Life-Conditioning: The Potteries Thinkbelt: A Plan for an Advanced Educational Industry in North Staffordshire," *Architectural Design* (October 1966): 483.

8   Cedric Price and Paul Barker, "The Potteries Thinkbelt," *New Society*, no. 2 (June 2, 1996): 15.

9   Mason White, "Disciplinary Thievery," *Oz*, vol. 34 (2012): 4.

10   Neeraj Bhatia, Maya Pryzbylski, Lola Sheppard and Mason White (Infranet Lab/Lateral Office), *Pamphlet Architecture 30: Coupling: Strategies for Infrastructural Opportunities* (New York: Princeton Architectural Press, 2011), 9.

11   Bhatia *et al.*, *Pamphlet Architecture 30*, 16.

12.1
View of the entrance,
Reiulf Ramstad Architects,
Trollstigplatået, Trollstigen,
Norway, 2010.

12

Case Study
Trollstigplatået—Trollstigen, Norway

The National Tourist Routes in Norway were developed by the Norwegian Public Roads Administration in conjunction with the Norwegian Tourist Board to capitalize on the country's unique (if sometimes difficult to access) natural features.[1] The eighteen scenic roads that currently make up the National Tourist Routes allow you to experience the awe and wonder of the natural setting at various destination points and along key routes. Like much of the country, many of the destinations along these routes are inaccessible by other methods of transportation, such as rail.

The routes create an elaborate network that links natural features all over the country and to each particular regions' culture, history and geology (Figure 12.2). This unified "brand" now preserves many of the older scenic meanders, while making the roads more accessible and visible to tourists. The project also provides much needed infrastructural improvements to the roads and new architecture that would serve as visitor centers, rest areas or other amenities.

A particularly unique feature of this large-scale undertaking is the way in which the infrastructural improvements have been tied to the cultivation of architecture. The government commissioned Norwegian architects, landscape architects and artists to design all of the routes' laybys, information points, and lookouts, and they are intended to showcase contemporary Norwegian architecture as a lens to the beauty of the natural terrain. Nearly all of the features that have been designed are as pragmatic and functional as they are artistic; for example, a piece of land art along one route also serves to protect from falling rocks, snow and ice.[2]

The Geiranger–Trollstigen National Tourist Route (Figure 12.3) runs from Sogge bru near Romsdal to Langevatn on the Strynefjell plateau over 106 km

12.2
Site diagram of the
National Tourist Routes
in Norway, linked by the
principal highways and
coastal ferries.

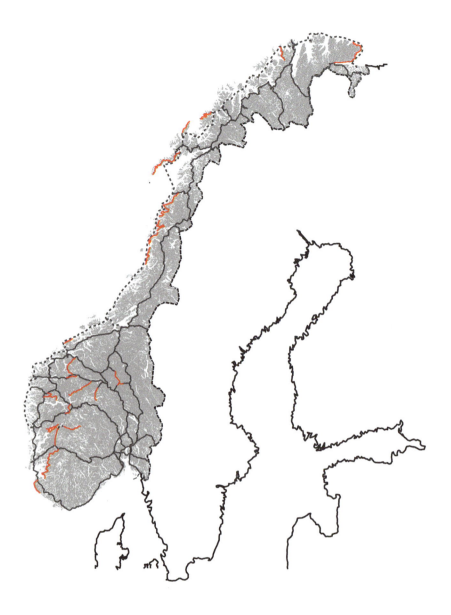

along the west coast of Norway in the county of Møre og Romsdal. The road meanders through part of what is known as "fjord country," which encompasses four counties on the west coast. The route takes you past the UNESCO-protected Geriangerfjord and across Storfjord by ferry to the Trollstigen Plateau and then down to the Ruama River. The historic Trollstigen road plunges down the mountain from the plateau at a 9 percent grade, with eleven hairpins to take you out into the valley. The road can currently only accommodate vehicles as long as 13.1 meters because of the hairpins, but with the improved infrastructure of the road, passing pockets have been incorporated to allow for better flow. Originally

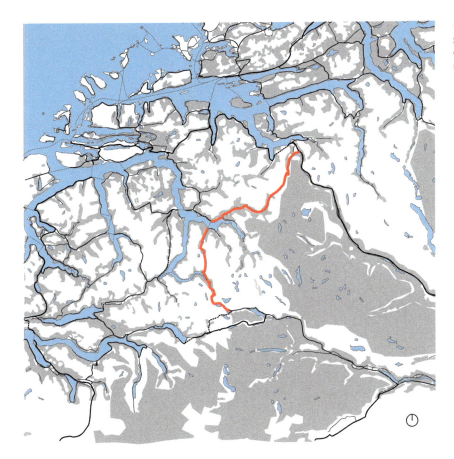

constructed in 1936, it continues to be accessible only from about June to
October.[3]

Reiulf Ramstad Architects won the invited competition for this feature and
was commissioned to design the Trollstigplatået—a visitor center, café, and
walking path system for the National Tourist Route at the Stigfossen Waterfall,
which sits on top of the Trollstigen Road. The visitor center and site exist as a kind
of topographical gateway and literal ledge from the Trollstigen Plateau to the
valley beyond. Despite the road being accessible for only a short time during the
summer months, the feature is one of the most trafficked destinations in Norway.

Defining the site was as much about carefully preserving the natural and
built systems flowing through the area as it was about framing the beauty of the
surroundings. Because of the immense effort taken to build the road, which is
literally inscribed into the slope of the mountain, people come not only to see the
beauty of the waterfalls and the valley, but also to see this infrastructural achieve-
ment meandering down the mountainside.

From the overall site plan (Figure 12.4), you begin to see the scale of Reiulf
Ramstad Architects' design emerge. It is difficult to consider the "whole" of the

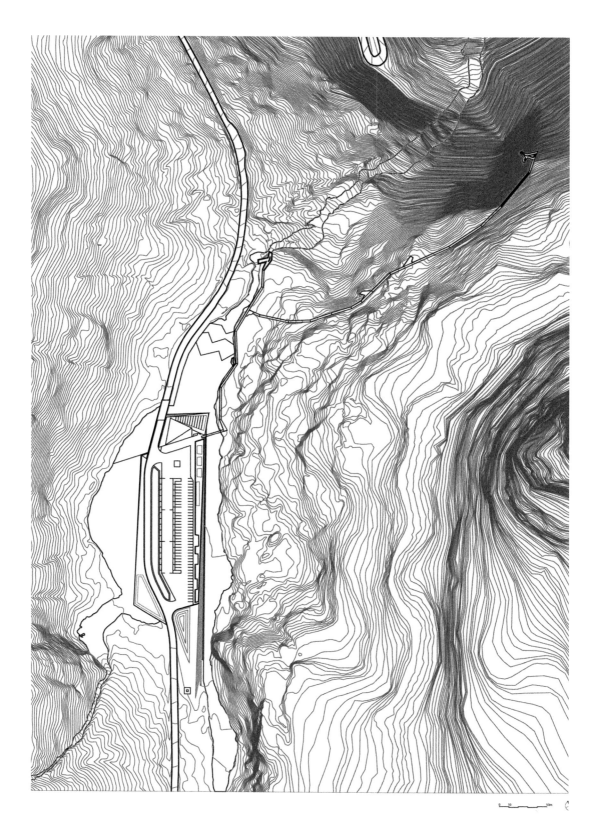

Systematizing Site

project as a contained and unified object—it is even difficult to put the entire scope of the project on a single plan. The site stretches between two mountains to the ledge where the waterfall drops off, tracing the flow of water, automobile traffic, and designated walking paths.

The visitor center lies directly on the path of water flowing off the mountain and nearby glaciers, which can be seen in the way the topography is leveled where the building and parking lot are located. The stream is channeled around the visitor center to link up with the existing mouth of the waterfall that spills off the precipice. The landscape architects Multiconsult were brought in to help design the system to control the flow, and with Reiulf Ramstad Architects they created a water feature that serves to prevent erosion and delay storm water, while providing two large retention ponds to look out on, walk by and view from the water's edge (Figure 12.6).

The flow of water is absolutely critical to the design of any feature for the area, given the extreme slopes as well as the amount of snowmelt in the summers. In the winter, the area can see up to 7 meters (over 22 feet) of snow— this is why the area must be closed seasonally. The structures built for the site had to support the snow loads for extended periods of time, which not only

12.4
[Opposite] Site plan, Reiulf Ramstad Architects, Trollstigplatået, Trollstigen, Norway, 2010.

12.5
View from above, Reiulf Ramstad Architects, Trollstigplatået, Trollstigen, Norway, 2010.

12.6
View of the retention
pond, Reiulf Ramstad
Architects, Trollstig-
platået, Trollstigen,
Norway, 2010.

impacted the structural character of the finished building, it also limited the timeframe in which construction could occur—because of this, the project took nearly seven years to complete.

Vehicular movement is another critical aspect of flow, shaping the architecture in relationship to its site. Trollstigplatået can receive upwards of 600,000 visitors during the summer, in around 100,000 cars.[4] Sufficient parking to accommodate a large number of visitors was required, and the parking area needed to be visible from the road without detracting from the beauty of the landscape. The parking area is placed in a direct relationship with the highway, using a traffic island planted with vegetation similar to the surroundings to pull visitors off of the route, allow ample room to park and maneuver, and still mask the parking area from the highway. While the parking area can seem overwhelmingly large on the site plan, it is still dwarfed by the scale of the natural features, and mitigated by the material choices for the landscaping. The retention pond visible from the highway is also at the scale of the parking area, working to visually balance the natural and built systems moving through the site.

The building that houses the visitor center is not only a gateway to the valley framed by the surrounding mountains; it is also a physical gateway to the pathways and viewpoints beyond. The architects chose to create a tectonic system (repeating and adapting materials and the way they are joined) for the entire project, helping to visually and architecturally link each part of the scheme

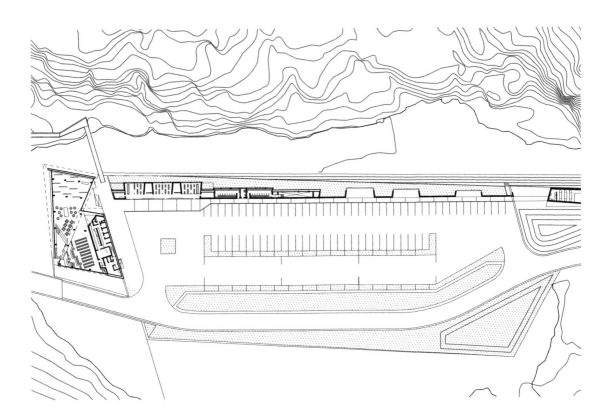

together. This unifying system is tied to a strong sense of procession as you make your way out of your car, into the building, and out into the landscape. The physical shape of the roofs of the visitor center channels you towards the entrance, reinforcing its nature as a threshold by framing the exterior landscape beyond the building. Part of the facility has been built into an artificial berm on the trailside of the visitor center, creating a threshold from your car to the walking path while obscuring the view back to the parking area.

The pathways beyond the visitor center navigate the complexities of the terrain and the problems of erosion by resting just above the ground. The paths skim the surface of the mountain, creating detours and benches along the way to engage with the water, while effectively relegating the traffic to a safe zone for the visitors as well as the ecology of the area. The trail structures weave the flow of water and the path of the visitors together and are designed to dramatize your experience of the surrounding area. Each destination is characterized by elaborating on the material palette introduced in the visitor center, shifting the tectonic sensibility to deal with each site-specific circumstance.

The first destination is modest: it allows you to dip close to the retention pond beyond the visitor center (Figure 12.8). A solid concrete platform glides above the surface of the water to bring you to its edge while attaching lightly to the pathway above. The second destination branches to another cantilevered viewing platform hovering over a large rock face, seemingly propped up by steel posts a few feet

12.7
Ground floor site plan, Reiulf Ramstad Architects, Trollstig-platået, Trollstigen, Norway, 2010.

12.8
View of the retention pond overlook, Reiulf Ramstad Architects, Trollstigplatået, Trollstigen, Norway, 2010.

above the stream as it flows towards the cliff (Figures 12.9–12.10). The balustrade characterizes this pathway: bands of Cor-ten steel pull apart to allow you to see past the barrier to the landscape beyond. The flora at this point on the trail is very close to your view, and the porous nature of the balustrade is critical for you to be able to engage in the environment immediately around you.

The final destination of the visitor path takes you twenty minutes along the cliff's edge to Stigfossen waterfall, which cascades over 1000 feet down the mountainside. The balustrade and pathway transition into a concrete walkway with a solid Cor-ten steel balustrade and concrete overlook—this is put in place because you are walking along the precipice edge and the views are to the grand panaroma beyond. The final viewpoint is architecturally and naturally more dramatic. You are literally perched out on an outcropping of steel and concrete to view the entire valley below you. At the very end of the viewpoint solid glass balustrades allow you the dizzying view immediately below your feet, making you realize how far you are suspended out over the cliff.

The systems in place on this site are complex, but by using an incredibly stripped-down tectonic palette the architecture can adapt to the existing conditions of the landscape while still providing for the ebb and flow of less predictable forces in the area, like crowds and storm water. The response is in many ways as infrastructural as the road network this destination is tied into.

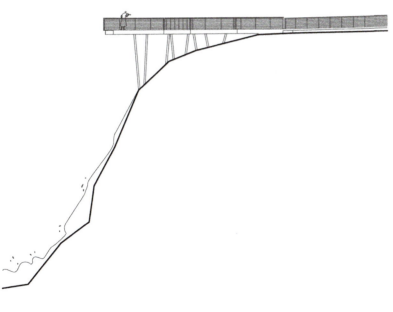

12.9
View of the panoramic
outlook, Reiulf Ramstad
Architects, Trollstig-
platået, Trollstigen,
Norway, 2010.

12.10
Elevation of the
panoramic outlook, Reiulf
Ramstad Architects,
Trollstigplatået,
Trollstigen, Norway,
2010.

0   2   10m

Case Study: Trollstigplatået—Trollstigen, Norway   **149**

12.11
View of the panoramic
platform, Reiulf Ramstad
Architects, Trollstig-
platået, Trollstigen,
Norway, 2010.

12.12
Elevation of the
panoramic platform,
Reiulf Ramstad
Architects, Trollstig-
platået, Trollstigen,
Norway, 2010.

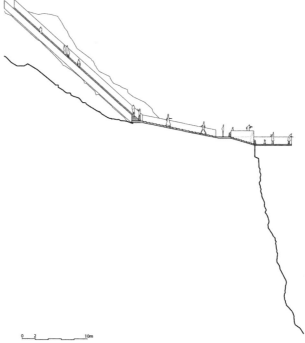

0   2   10m

Basic tectonic elements are repeated and recombined to change your experience as the visitor, adapting to the varying geological features. The strength of the project lies in its infrastructure. It must be navigated: your experience through the site is also your experience of the architecture, which depends on the delicate balance between the built and natural systems.

Notes

1   Ellen Njøs Slinde, "Sognefjellet national tourist road," *Topos* (2004): 123–135, www.veg vesen.no/_attachment/160955/binary/299526?fast_title=2004+Topos+-+artikkel+ om+turistvegar.pdf.

2   Karl Otto Ellefsen, "Detoured Infrastructure: The Architecture of the National Tourist Routes," in *Detour: Architecture and Design along 18 National Tourist Routes in Norway*, ed. Nina Berre and Hege Lysholm (Shanghai: Promus Printing, 2010), 20.

3   Norwegian Public Roads Administration, "Geiranger-Trollstigen," www.nasjonaletur- istveger.no/stream_file.asp?iEntityId=2687.

4   Reiulf Ramstad Architects, "Trollstigen National Tourist Route Project," fact sheet, October 31, 2013.

Afterword

The preceding chapters are an attempt to capture an idea of what site *is* relative to architecture. While hopefully evident in the projects illustrated, where site ends and architecture begins is not as clearly demarcated as the two terms might suggest, even though the entire book has been devoted to the definition, representation, interpretation, and understanding of site in architecture and by architects.

Site is not a term exclusive to architecture, and it occupies a contentious zone as the term (and the design field) expands and blurs between objects and their surroundings. Other disciplines lay claim to this territory, including urban design, planning, and landscape architecture. Site is itself an interpretation of the surroundings to frame a project, but its role is subject to different perceptions within architecture and between the disciplines, leading to a critical moment in the term's meaning.

One perception of site is as an entirely distinct entity from architecture: it depends on the architect designing the object, the landscape architect designing the site, and the planners knitting these objects and sites together (Figure 13.1). This neatly defines the roles of each field, but the division is rarely this simple to allocate, and there are almost always exceptions. The perception also undermines the notion that architecture has a connection or relevance to its site. It can imply

SITE	ARCHITECTURE

13.1
Site as a distinct entity from architecture.

that architects are solely responsible for the object they make, not the consequences of it in its environment. Most architects would invariably disagree that they deliberately ignore the site and its development, especially given the effects the built environment has on our climate and the world. However, the division between landscape architecture, planning and architecture has come about in some sense because architects have been asked to neglect the site, leaving open the opportunity for others to appropriate and privilege it.

The perceived distance between site and architecture is unfortunately exacerbated in academia, where it is an all too common occurrence for students to learn design by ignoring or refusing to take ownership of the site, creating digital and physical models divorced from the location it will be placed into, or site plans peppered with tree symbols to indicate landscape, no topography, and little notion that the exterior is part of their design. This is not to accuse or to blame students or faculty, but to acknowledge that this perception often begins in school and is then propagated in the profession. There is quite a lot to think about when designing architecture. This sentiment is echoed in the book *Siteless*, by architect François Blanciak, who advocates for the consideration of form before site: "The traditional sequence 'program plus site equals form' is here intentionally inverted: as in ancient column orders, schemes are conceived prior to site insertion and subsequent relationships and adaptations."[1] For Blanciak, it is easier to invent form disassociated from its site (while ironically the forms that make up his book are organized by their place of inception). The site is perceived to be over there, away from the architecture: its form is "inserted" into site.

13.2
Site as an exclusive piece of architecture.

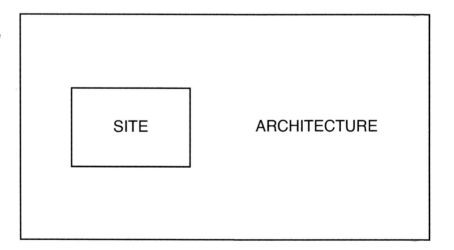

Another perception of site is as a contained element within the practice of architecture: a site is a part of the sequence of designing a building (Figure 13.2). This relegates all understanding of site conditions, site planning, and any poetic notion of the place to a fixed point along the path to a finished project. The perception limits the role of site to its legal implications related to planning, grading, zoning and design.[2] Again, and without faulting any particular party, this is exacerbated in academia, where courses in site planning, for instance, attempt to address these site categories as a set of fixed rules and potentially pedantic methods that can be assessed on multiple-choice exams, further reinforced through the process of registration. The perception is useful to the profession because it establishes the minimum amount of information necessary to legally build a piece of architecture, but it can lead to a tick-in-the-box approach to site that willfully packages what may be dynamic, changeable and unfixed about a place into readily accessible information packets that can be applied to a building.

Sculpture, in its relationship to site, has gone through its own ontological crisis, more easily defined by what it was not. Rosalind Krauss, looking at the transformation of sculpture from the 1960s to the 1970s, remarked on the state the term "sculpture" had reached: "We had thought to use a universal category to authenticate a group of particulars, but the category has now been forced to cover such a heterogeneity that it is, itself, in danger of collapsing."[3] For Krauss, it was necessary to describe an expanded field based on sculpture's transforming relationship to site to better categorize those works of art that could not easily fit the term "sculpture." This field is "generated by problematizing the set of oppositions between which the modernist category *sculpture* is suspended."[4]

A third perception of site exists in a similarly expanded field, with potentially less structure than that outlined by Krauss (Figure 13.3). Intersections, overlaps, hybridizations and emerging trajectories can now be seen between landscape architecture, land art, infrastructure, sustainability, ecology, urban design, planning, and architecture—all of which revolve around notions of the site. Similar to the outpouring of "-isms" arising out of modern art, terms have been hybridized, verbs converted to gerunds, and colors now define whole movements. The

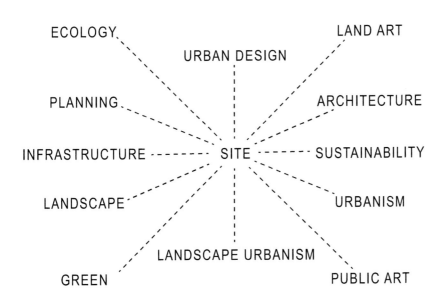

13.3
Site at the core of all existing and emerging disciplines and movements.

perception of site at the center of this crossbreeding of disciplines and movements is highly encouraging to open the doors of invention, and it places the significance of site relative to any human occupation on the land firmly at the origin of these existing and emerging fields.

Yet the lack of structure that organizes this bonanza of term-making runs the risk of losing all criticality regarding the site as a design that builds on a lineage of approaches, methods and attitudes inherent to each discipline. This perception of site, like that of sculpture, is too heterogeneous: site will lose its meaning by attempting to be suspended between a set of similarities, blurring distinctions, and non-oppositions as the disciplines subdivide, recombine and appropriate territory from each other to generate new ideas and re-categorize themselves relative to each other.

13.4
Site as an integral part
of architecture.

SITE   ARCHITECTURE

A last perception of a site exists in relative ambiguity, relying on the properties of its representation (Figure 13.4). Like walking into a fog, you may know it when you are in it, and you may catch a trace of it as you walk towards it, but site in this sense does not have clearly defined edges: it is a collective notion of individual interpretations based on the way in which site is drawn. Robin Evans describes a "suspension of critical disbelief" necessary for architects to create drawings that will translate into buildings, but "a curious situation has come to pass in which ... the *properties* of drawing—its peculiar powers in relation to its putative subject, the building—are hardly recognized at all."[5]

The *properties* of drawing are the key to this perception of site: it entails a process by which a place transforms into the way in which it will create the project. This is not to suggest that site is subservient to architecture but to recognize that it is bound up with the making of architecture. This perception is multivalent, and open-ended without precluding other perceptions of the term site listed above, but it centers on acknowledging what Evans also describes as "an enabling fiction."[6] The representation of a design is a fiction of what will be built, but it enables the process of its construction. Similarly, the representation of a site is a fiction of what is *there*, but it enables the process of design.

The larger project of the book seeks a kind of elusive DNA at the core of architecture relative to site (in opposition to, intertwined with, blurring the distinction between, etc.) that can proliferate seemingly infinite variations within controlled limits and following a broad history of precedents. Site—its definition and representation—should be a self-reflexive and self-aware activity. This may, as the increasing number of inter-disciplines already demonstrate, open the doors to invention by acknowledging the role site plays, while preserving the meaning of the term as an essential enabling fiction in architecture.

Notes

1   Francois Blançiak, *Siteless: 1001 Building Forms* (Cambridge, MA: MIT Press, 2008), ix.

2   This is a reference to the current National Council of Architectural Registration Board's Architectural Registration Exam categories, where the site is characterized and applicable zoning established in the Programming, Planning and Practice Exam, and site grading, planning and design is outlined in the Site Planning and Design Exam. For more information, see www.ncarb.org/ARE/Taking-the-ARE/ARE4-Divisions.aspx.

3   Rosalind Krauss, "Sculpture in the Expanded Field," in her *The Originality of the Avant-Garde and Other Modernist Myths* (Cambridge, MA: MIT Press, 1985), 279.

4   Krauss, "Sculpture," 284.

5   Robin Evans, "Translations from Drawing to Building," in his *Translations from Drawing to Building and Other Essays* (London: Architectural Association, 1997), 154.

6   Evans, "Translations," 154.

Further Reading

Allen, Stan. *Points and Lines: Diagrams and Projects for the City.* **New York: Princeton Architectural Press, 1999.**

This book presents several projects and texts by Stan Allen, who is both an academic and architect, with an introduction by K. Michael Hays. While a portion of his text is referred to in the first chapter of *Interpreting Site*, his book offers more insight into his overall project—how his thinking and writing translate into his design work. The book is structured by introducing essays according to specific theoretical ideas—contextual tactics, infrastructural urbanism and field conditions—followed by architectural projects related to the larger conceptual idea.

Burns, Carol J. and Andrea Kahn (editors). *Site Matters: Design Concepts, Histories, and Strategies.* **New York: Routledge, 2005.**

This collection of primarily text-based essays offers a broad range of voices that seek to shape a contemporary discourse on site as the object of design. The authors included in this book come from varied backgrounds including art criticism, urban planning and policy, architecture, landscape architecture, urban design, ecology, architectural practice, and geography. Two essays from this collection are referred to in *Interpreting Site*, but all offer valuable insight into larger notions of site that bridge between disciplines.

Cook, Peter. *Drawing: The Motive Force of Architecture.* **New York: John Wiley & Sons, 2008.**

This book centers on the act, nature, purpose and potential of drawing in all its various incarnations from sketching to digitalization. It is an effective primer or introduction to the making of architecture that provides a large amount of visual material at varying stages of the design process and across a broad range of individual designers and mediums. The writing accompanying the imagery is accessible, especially for students, and anecdotal, focusing on the creation of architecture as fundamentally tied to the production of drawing.

Corner, James (editor). *Recovering Landscape: Essays in Contemporary Landscape Architecture.* **New York: Princeton Architectural Press, 1999.**

This collection of essays addresses a renewed interest in landscape and the important directions for landscape practices in the future gathered from two symposiums and invited essays, including all disciplines. The term "landscape" is intentionally expansive for the purposes of this book to include urbanism, infrastructure, strategic planning, and more speculative notions of the term. The essays are highly relevant to the architectural discipline and are structured in three sections: Reclaiming Place and Time, Constructing and Representing the Landscape (including essays that address issues related to the representation of site), and Urbanizing Landscape (exploring environments where landscape and architecture are distinctly blurred).

Cosgrove, Denis. *Apollo's Eye: A Cartographic Genealogy of the Earth in the Western Imagination.* **Baltimore, MD: Johns Hopkins University Press, 2001.**

This book explores the historical implications of what we understand as Western civilization by conceiving and representing the earth as a spherical form. The title refers to the vantage point necessary (through Apollo's eye) to construct this notion of the globe. The book covers a genealogy from ancient Greece and Rome to the twentieth century of global images (from maps, photographs, and other representations) and meanings (globe, earth and world, for example). These collective conceptions of the earth underpin any individual interpretation of site, from the phenomenological to the representational, but are frequently taken for granted, and a book devoted to the topic is highly relevant to any consideration of site.

Evans, Robin. *Translations from Drawing to Building and Other Essays.* **London: Architectural Association, 1997.**

This book is a posthumous collection of the writings of Robin Evans, architectural historian, theorist, and architect, with an introduction by Moshen Mostafavi, and a chronology of his writings by Robin Middleton. Particularly interesting in this collection is his critical essay on the Barcelona Pavilion, as well as the essays on his concern in uncovering the possibilities in representation, from projection to drawings, in architecture. "Translations from Drawing to Building" is of specific relevance to understanding the nature of the drawing in architecture and how it shapes the discipline distinct from the arts.

Frampton, Kenneth. "Towards a Critical Regionalism: Six Points for an Architecture of Resistance." In *The Anti-Aesthetic: Essays on Postmodern Culture*, edited by Hal Foster, 16–30. Port Townsend, WA: Bay Press, 1983.

This essay outlines what Frampton considers as the problem of universalization in the modern world, and the need for a rear-guard approach to architecture to restore its relationship to site and its significance to society. Topography, context, climate, light and tectonic form are the key factors that contribute to a buildings idiosyncratic relationship to its site. This seminal work is especially critical to read in relationship to his larger book *Studies in Tectonic Culture*, where his thesis on tectonic form emerges.

Frampton, Kenneth. *Studies in Tectonic Culture: The Poetics of Construction in Nineteenth and Twentieth Century Architecture*, edited by John Cava. Cambridge, MA: MIT Press, 1995.

This book examines the history of tectonics as a theoretical concept developed initially in the nineteenth century understanding architecture as a mediation and articulation of the poetic and cognitive aspects of its substance. Frampton's focus is on the relationship of the heavy and the light in tectonics, which fundamentally revolves around the origins of architecture in its relationship to its site, the earth. The book moves from the historical development of the tectonic as an idea to the exploration of works by the architects Frank Lloyd Wright, Auguste Perret, Mies van der Rohe, Louis Kahn, Jørn Utzon and Carlo Scarpa. The Poscriptum offers an encapsulated history of the development of tectonics in architecture through the twentieth century and its future trajectories.

Frascari, Marco, Jonathan Hale, Bradley Starkey (editors). *From Models to Drawings: Imagination and Representation in Architecture*. New York: Routledge, 2008.

This collection of essays stem from the conference Models and Drawing: The Invisible Nature of Architecture, in reaction to the present conditions of architectural modelling and drawing, especially in relation to the problems faced with digital media, but also as the drawing becomes an art piece rather than an essential part of the production of design. The essays all investigate the processes of architectural representation to provoke unseen visions, from historical perspectives of drawing and model making to the limits of the digital and moving image, as well as critical thinking on the role of the model and the drawing in emerging representational methods.

Krauss, Rosalind. *The Originality of the Avant-Garde and Other Modernist Myths*. Cambridge, MA: MIT Press, 1985.

This book is a collection of writings by art critic Rosalind Krauss. These essays were written from 1973 to 1983, and can be seen as not only the evolution of an essential critical voice in the art world, but also the development of that art world.

Much of her work ultimately revolves around the question of meaning in art as the nature and medium of art has transformed, examining the artist's intentions as well as the way in which we make sense of the contemporary production of art, questioning the nature of criticism.

Leupen, Bernard, Christoph Grafe, Nicola Körnig, Mark Lampe, Peter de Zeeuw, and Jan Verbeek. *Design and Analysis.* **Amsterdam: 010 Publishers, 1997.**

This book seeks to show how analysis and representation are used in all aspects of architecture to influence the design itself, effectively linking representational method with design. It offers strong and clearly written insight into the aspects of analysis throughout design, such as order and composition, use, context, typology, and structure. The visuals, while all black and white, are well chosen, show a great variety in representational systems and approaches without offering step-by-step methods, and work between existing drawings by architects and those drawn for the book's purpose.

Lynch, Kevin and Gary Hack. *Site Planning,* **3rd edition. Cambridge, MA: MIT Press, 1984.**

This textbook comprehensively covers the breadth of ways in which site enters into the design and implementation of architecture. The text touches on all aspects relating to site, including representation, larger cultural context and particularly pragmatic and professional concerns. It is accessibly written and provides a self-described exposition of principles and condensed technical reference that can easily be used as such, both in school and in the profession. The chapters are thematic, first covering the process of design, then into specific topics in materials, access, earthwork, and utilities. There is also a large appendix to the text that offers detailed technical information related to soils, sun angles, noise, landscaping types, climate, surveying and costing.

Unwin, Simon. *Analysing Architecture,* **3rd edition. London: Routledge, 2009.**

While a portion of this text is referred to in the first chapter of *Interpreting Site*, Unwin's book offers a much broader range of strategies and discussion to introduce the fundamental elements and concepts of architectural design. Relying on the author's illustrations to illuminate the text, the book links analysis to the design of architecture through place and place-making, seeking to understand the intellectual processes underpinning architecture without prescribing specific process.

Bibliography

Abraham, Raimund. "Negation and Reconciliation." In *Theorizing a New Agenda for Architecture: An Anthology of Architectural Theory 1965–1995*, edited by Kate Nesbitt, 464–465. New York: Princeton Architectural Press, 1996.

Alberti, Leon Battista. *On the Art of Building in Ten Books*. Translated by J. Rykwert, N. Leach, and R. Tavernor. Cambridge, MA: MIT Press, 1988.

Allen, Stan. "Field Conditions." In his *Points and Lines: Diagrams and Projects for the City*, 92–103. New York: Princeton Architectural Press, 1999.

Allen, Stan. "Mapping the Unmappable: On Notation." In his *Practice: Architecture, Technique and Representation*, 31–45. Amsterdam: Overseas Publishers Association, 2000.

Ando, Tadao. "Toward New Horizons in Architecture." In *Theorizing a New Agenda for Architecture: An Anthology of Architectural Theory 1965–1995*, edited by Kate Nesbitt, 458–461. New York: Princeton Architectural Press, 1996.

Banham, Reyner. *Los Angeles: The Architecture of Four Ecologies*. London: Penguin, 1971.

Beauregard, Robert. "From Place to Site: Negotiating Narrative Complexity." In *Site Matters: Design Concepts, Histories, and Strategies*, edited by Carol J. Burns and Andrea Kahn, 39–58. New York: Routledge, 2005.

Bhatia, Neeraj, Maya Pryzbylski, Lola Sheppard and Mason White (Infranet Lab/Lateral Office). *Pamphlet Architecture 30: Coupling: Strategies for Infrastructural Opportunities*. New York: Princeton Architectural Press, 2011.

Blançiak, Francois. *Siteless: 1001 Building Forms*. Cambridge, MA: MIT Press, 2008.

Borges, Jorge Luis. "On Exactitude in Science." In his *Collected Fictions*, translated by Andrew Hurley, 325. New York: Penguin, 1999.

Corner, James. "Eidetic Operations and New Landscapes." In *Recovering Landscape: Essays in Contemporary Landscape Architecture*, edited by James Corner, 153–170. New York: Princeton Architectural Press, 1999.

Cosgrove, Denis. *Apollo's Eye: A Cartographic Genealogy of the Earth in the Western Imagination*. Baltimore, MD: Johns Hopkins University Press, 2001.

Cosgrove, Denis. "The Measures of America." In *Taking Measures Across the American Landscape*, by James Corner and Alex MacLean, 3–13. New Haven, CT: Yale University Press, 1996.

de Certeau, Michel. *Practice of Everyday Life*, translated by Steven Rendall. Berkeley, CA: University of California Press, 1984.

Deleuze, Gilles. "Rhizome Versus Trees." In *The Deleuze Reader*, edited by Constanin V. Boundas, 27–36. New York: Columbia University Press, 1993.

Denari, Neil M. *Gyroscopic Horizons*. New York: Princeton Architectural Press, 1999.

Dripps, Robin. "Groundwork." In *Site Matters: Design Concepts, Histories, and Strategies*, edited by Andrea Kahn and Carol J. Burns, 59–91. New York: Routledge, 2005.

Eames, Charles and Ray. *Powers of Ten*, documentary short film, directed and written by Charles and Ray Eames, 1968. DVD: Chatsworth, CA: Image Entertainment, 2000.

Ellefsen, Karl Otto. "Detoured Infrastructure: The Architecture of the National Tourist Routes." In *Detour: Architecture and Design along 18 National Tourist Routes in Norway*, edited by Nina Berre and Hege Lysholm, 17–27. Shanghai: Promus Printing, 2010.

Evans, Robin. "Translations from Drawing to Building." In his *Translations from Drawing to Building and Other Essays*, 152–193. London: Architectural Association, 1997.

Ferriss, Hugh. *Power in Buildings: An Artist's View of Contemporary Architecture*. Santa Monica, CA: Hennessey + Ingalls, 1998.

Frampton, Kenneth. *Álvaro Siza: the Complete Works*. London: Phaidon Press, 2000.

Frampton, Kenneth. "Towards a Critical Regionalism: Six Points for an Architecture of Resistance." In *The Anti-Aesthetic: Essays on Postmodern Culture*, edited by Hal Foster, 16–30. Port Townsend, WA: Bay Press, 1983.

Frascari, Marco. *Eleven Exercises in the Art of Architectural Drawing: Slow Food for the Architect's Imagination*. London: Routledge, 2011.

Frascari, Marco. "The Tell-the-Tale Detail." In *Theorizing a New Agenda for Architecture: An Anthology of Architectural Theory 1965–1995*, edited by Kate Nesbitt, 498–515. New York: Princeton Architectural Press, 1996.

Fuller, R. Buckminster. *Nine Chains to the Moon*. Carbondale, IL: Southern Illinois University Press and Feffer & Simons, 1938.

Garcia, Mark. "Introduction: Histories and Theories of the Diagrams of Architecture." In *The Diagrams of Architecture: A Reader*, edited by Mark Garcia, 18–45. Chichester: John Wiley & Sons, 2010.

Gregotti, Vittorio. *Architecture: Means and Ends*, translated by Lydia G. Cochrane. Chicago, IL: University of Chicago Press, 2010.

Guildin, James M. "A History of Forest Management in the Ozark Mountains." In *Pioneer Forest—A Half Century of Sustainable Uneven-aged Forest Management in the Missouri Ozark*, by James M Guldin, Greg F. Iffrig, and Susan L. Flader, 3–8. General Technical Report, SRS108. Asheville, NC: U.S. Department of Agriculture, Forest Service, Southern Research Station, 2008.

Heidegger, Martin. "Building Dwelling Thinking." In his *Poetry, Language, Thought*, translated by A. Hofstadter, 145–161. New York: Harper & Row, 1971.

Holl, Steven. *Anchoring*. New York: Princeton Architectural Press, 1989.

Holl, Steven. *Pamphlet Architecture 5: The Alphabetical City*. New York: Pamphlet Architecture and William Stout Architectural Books, 1980.

Holl, Steven. *Pamphlet Architecture 13: Edge of a City*. New York: Princeton Architectural Press and Pamphlet Architecture, 1991.

Johnson, Steven. *Emergence: The Connected Lives of Ants, Brains, Cities and Software*. New York: Scribner, 2001.

Johnson, Steven. *The Ghost Map: The Story of London's Most Terrifying Epidemic—and How It Changed Science, Cities and the Modern World*. New York: Riverhead Books, 2006.

Kahn, Louis I. "Toward a Plan for Midtown Philadelphia." *Perspecta*, vol. 2 (1953): 10–27.

Kaijima, Momoyo, Junzo Kuroda, and Yoshiharu Tsukamoto. *Made in Tokyo*. Tokyo: Kajima Institute Publishing, 2001.

Krauss, Rosalind. "Sculpture in the Expanded Field." In her *The Originality of the Avant-Garde and Other Modernist Myths*, 276–290. Cambridge, MA: MIT Press, 1985.

Lucan, Jacques, ed. *OMA–Rem Koolhaas: Architecture, 1970–1990*, translated by David Block. New York: Princeton Architectural Press, 1991.

Lynch, Kevin and Gary Hack. *Site Planning*, 3rd edition. Cambridge, MA: MIT Press, 1984.

Maas, Winy and MVRDV. *Metacity/Datatown*. Rotterdam: MVRDV/010 Publishers, 1999.

Marks, Robert W. *The Dymaxion World of Buckminster Fuller*. New York: Reinhold Publishing Corporation, 1960.

Mathur, Anuradha and Dilip da Cunha. "The Sea and Monsoon Within: A Mumbai Manifesto." In *Ecological Urbanism*, edited by Mohsen Mostafavi and Gareth Doherty, 194–201. Baden: Lars Mueller Publishers with Harvard University, Graduate School of Design, 2010–2011.

Mead, Christopher C. *Roadcut: The Architecture of Antoine Predock*. Albuquerque, NM: University of New Mexico Press, 2011.

Mead, Christopher C. "Sighting the Landscape." In *Antoine Predock*, by Antoine Predock, 8–23. Seoul: C3 Design Group, 2001.

Pallasmaa, Juhanni. *The Thinking Hand: Existential and Embodied Wisdom in Architecture*. Chichester: John Wiley & Sons, 2009.

Price, Cedric. "Life-Conditioning: The Potteries Thinkbelt: A plan for an advanced educational industry in North Staffordshire." *Architectural Design* (October 1966): 483–497.

Price, Cedric and Paul Barker. "The Potteries Thinkbelt." *New Society*, no. 2 (June 2, 1996): 15.

Rashid, Hani and Lise Anne Couture. *Asymptote: Architecture at the Interval*. New York: Rizzoli International Publications and Asymptote Architecture, 1995.

Richter, Dagmar. *XYZ: The Architecture of Dagmar Richter*. London: Laurence King Publishing, 2001.

Robinson, Arthur Howard. *Which Map is Best? Projections for World Maps*. Falls Church, VA: American Congress on Surveying and Mapping, 1986.

Rowe, Colin and Fred Koetter. *Collage City*. Cambridge, MA: MIT Press, 1979.

Siza, Álvaro. *Siza: Architecture Writings*, edited by Antonio Angelillo. Milan: Skira, 1997.

Somol, Robert E. "Dummy Text, or The Diagrammatic Basis of Contemporary Architecture." In *Diagram Diaries*, by Peter Eisenman, 6–25. New York: Universe Publishing, 1999.

Stalder, Laurent. "Projection of the Mind and Protection of the Body." In *Projects and Architecture: Dominique Perrault*, translated by Christopher Evans, edited by Giovanna Crespi, 7–27. Milan: Electa Architecture, 2000.

Taylor, Brandon. *Collage: The Making of Modern Art*. New York: Thames & Hudson, 2004.

Tuomey, John. *Architecture, Craft and Culture: Reflections on the Work of O'Donnell +Tuomey*. Edge Series—Ideas on Art and Architecture. Cork: Gandon Editions, 2004.

Unwin, Simon. *Analysing Architecture*, 3rd edition. London: Routledge, 2009.

Venturi, Robert, Denise Scott Brown and Steven Izenour. *Learning from Las Vegas: The Forgotten Symbolism of Architectural Form*, revised edition. Cambridge, MA: MIT Press, 1977.

Westerbeck, Colin and Joel Meyerowitz. *Bystander: A History of Street Photography*. Boston, MA: Little, Brown & Company, 2001.

White, Mason. "Disciplinary Thievery." *Oz*, vol. 34 (2012): 4–13.

Wigglesworth, Sarah and Jeremy Till. "Table Manners." In *The Everyday and Architecture*, Architectural Design Profile no. 134, edited by Sarah Wigglesworth and Jeremy Till, 31–36. London: Academy Editions, 1998.

Image Credits

1.1–1.4   Image courtesy of Simon Unwin.

1.5   Image courtesy of Stanley Allen.

1.6   Genevieve Baudoin.

1.7   From J. L. Kingston, *The Skyscraper: A Study in the Economic Height of Modern Office Buildings* (Chicago, IL: American Institute of Steel Construction, 1930), 15. Copyright © American Institute of Steel Construction. Reprinted with permission. All rights reserved.

1.8–1.11   Genevieve Baudoin.

1.12   Image courtesy of OMA (Office of Metropolitan Architecture), Heer Bokelweg 149, 3032 AD Rotterdam, Netherlands (www.oma.eu).

2.1   Image courtesy of Richard Meier & Partners.

2.2   Image courtesy of Renzo Piano Building Workshop. Credits: Otranto Urban Regeneration Workshop. Client: UNESCO (S. Busutill, W. Tochtermann). Studio Piano & Rice. Consultants: Ove Arup & Partners, IDEA Institute, G. P. Cuppini, G. Gasbarri, Editech; G. F. Dioguardi (coordination and administration).

2.3   Image courtesy of Steven Holl Architects.

2.4   From Enric Miralles, ed. Benedetta Tagliabue, *Enric Miralles: Works and Projects, 1975–1995* (New York: Monacelli Press, 1996). Image by Enric Miralles © Miralles Tagliabue EMBT.

2.5   Image courtesy of Neil M. Denari Architects, Inc.

2.6–2.7   Image courtesy of Dagmar Richter.

2.8   From Kurt Forster, Jacques Derrida, Bernhard Schneider and Mark C. Taylor, *Daniel Libeskind: radix-matrix: Architecture and Writings* (New York: Prestel, 1997). Image by Studio Daniel Libsekind ©

	1997 Prestel Verlag, by permission of Studio Daniel Libeskind and Prestel Verlag.
3.1	Image courtesy of Amann-Cánovas-Maruri, photo by David Frutos
3.2	Genevieve Baudoin.
3.3	Image courtesy of Amann-Cánovas-Maruri.
3.4–3.5	Image courtesy of Amann-Cánovas-Maruri, photo by David Frutos.
3.6–3.11	Image courtesy of Amann-Cánovas-Maruri.
3.12	Image courtesy of Amann-Cánovas-Maruri, photo by David Frutos.
4.1–4.3	From James Corner and Alex MacLean, *Taking Measures Across the American Landscape* (New haven, CT: Yale University Press, 1996), image by James Corner © 1996 Yale University Press, by permission of James Corner and Yale University Press.
4.4	Galerie Berinson, Berlin. © 2014 Artists Rights Society (ARS), New York/VG Bild-Kunst, Bonn.
4.5–4.6	Image courtesy of Antoine Predock Architect PC.
5.1–5.4	Image courtesy of Álvaro Siza 2—Arquitecto, SA.
5.5	© Dominique Perrault/Adagp.
5.6–5.7	© DPA/Adagp.
5.8	© Dominique Perrault/DPA/Adagp.
5.9–5.10	© DPA/Adagp.
5.11–5.12	Image courtesy of Anuradha Mathur and Dilip da Cunha.
6.1	Image courtesy of Bruce A. Johnson.
6.2–6.3	Genevieve Baudoin, adapted from USGS maps.
6.4–6.11	Image courtesy of Bruce A. Johnson.
7.1–7.2	From Colin Rowe and Fred Koetter, *Collage City* (Cambridge, MA: MIT Press, 1979), drawing by Wayne Copper, 62. © 1979 Massachusetts Institute of Technology, by permission of The MIT Press.
7.3–7.6	Genevieve Baudoin.
7.7	From Robert Venturi, Denise Scott Brown, and Steven Izenour, *Learning from Las Vegas: The Forgotten Symbolism of Architectural Form*, revised edition (Cambridge, MA: MIT Press, 1977). The Architectural Archives, University of Pennsylvania, by the gift of Robert Venturi and Denise Scott Brown.
8.1	Genevieve Baudoin.
8.2–8.3	From Robert Venturi, Denise Scott Brown, and Steven Izenour, *Learning from Las Vegas: The Forgotten Symbolism of Architectural Form*, revised edition (Cambridge, MA: MIT Press, 1977). The Architectural Archives, University of Pennsylvania, by the gift of Robert Venturi and Denise Scott Brown.
8.4–8.7	From Momoyo Kaijima, Junzo Kuroda, and Yoshiharu Tsukamoto, *Made in Tokyo* (Tokyo: Kajima Institute Publishing, 2001), by permission of Atelier Bow Wow and Kajima Institute Publishing.
9.1–9.2	Image courtesy of O'Donnell + Tuomey Ltd.

Index